THE ABUNDANCE WITHIN

Wealth, Happiness and Fulfillment in every aspect of Life

DR. PARNAVI GANATRA

Chennai • Bangalore

CLEVER FOX PUBLISHING
Chennai, India

Published by CLEVER FOX PUBLISHING 2025
Copyright © DR. PARNAVI GANATRA 2025

All Rights Reserved.
ISBN: 978-93-67070-11-6

This book has been published with all reasonable efforts taken to make the material error-free after the consent of the author. No part of this book shall be used, reproduced in any manner whatsoever without written permission from the author, except in the case of brief quotations embodied in critical articles and reviews.

The Author of this book is solely responsible and liable for its content including but not limited to the views, representations, descriptions, statements, information, opinions and references ["Content"]. The Content of this book shall not constitute or be construed or deemed to reflect the opinion or expression of the Publisher or Editor. Neither the Publisher nor Editor endorse or approve the Content of this book or guarantee the reliability, accuracy or completeness of the Content published herein and do not make any representations or warranties of any kind, express or implied, including but not limited to the implied warranties of merchantability, fitness for a particular purpose. The Publisher and Editor shall not be liable whatsoever for any errors, omissions, whether such errors or omissions result from negligence, accident, or any other cause or claims for loss or damages of any kind, including without limitation, indirect or consequential loss or damage arising out of use, inability to use, or about the reliability, accuracy or sufficiency of the information contained in this book.

DEDICATION

To the dreamers and doers,
To those who refuse to settle for less than their true potential,
To the seekers of joy, fulfillment, love and abundance,
This book is dedicated to you.
May it serve as a guiding light on your journey to discover The Abundance Within.

INSPIRATIONAL CALL TO ACTION

"This book is not just about reading; it's about transformation. Let it guide you to discover your untapped potential and align with the abundance within you."

"Within your heart, a spark does glow,

The seeds of joy, where dreams do grow.

Abundance whispers, "Seek, and you'll find,"

The power resides within your mind."

READER'S INTENTION PAGE

"My intentions for Reading This Book."

*I*n this blank page please write your goals, your limiting beliefs that you want to overcome, your purpose, your relations, your needs and much more to transform your life.

ACKNOWLEDGMENT AND GRATITUDE

First and foremost, I extend my deepest gratitude to the universe for its infinite wisdom and guiding me through this journey of self-discovery and growth. Writing *The Abundance Within* has been a transformative experience and I am grateful for the insights and lessons that life has offered me along the way.

To my family, friends and loved ones, your unwavering support, encouragement and belief in me have been my anchor throughout this process. Thank you for being pillars of strength.

I wish to express my heartfelt appreciation to all the spiritual teachers, authors and mentors, both those I have met personally and those whose wisdom I have drawn through books, podcasts and teachings all these years. Your knowledge and inspiration have helped me weave the essence of abundance into this book.

A special thank you to my readers, who are embarking on this journey of self-discovery and abundance with me. Your belief in the power of personal growth and transformation fuels my passion for writing.

ACKNOWLEDGMENT AND GRATITUDE

Lastly, to the team of editors, designers, publishing professionals and various platforms who have helped bring this book to life, your dedication and hard work are truly invaluable.

Thank you all for being part of this beautiful journey.

CONTENTS

THE ABUNDANCE WITHIN: WEALTH, HAPPINESS AND FULFILLMENT IN EVERY ASPECT OF LIFE xii

Introduction xiii

1. Mindset Matters 1

2. Breaking Free From Limiting Beliefs..........................10

3. Self Love and Acceptance 15

4. The Power of Relationships 25

5. The Beautiful Balance of Yin and Yang: Masculine and Feminine Energy 35

6. Overcoming Challenges With Grace 41

7. Leadership Mindset- Awaken the Leader Within You...46

8. Financial Wellness and Abundance Mindset...............51

9. What if Money Was A Person? 60

10. Mindfulness and Being Present 65

CONTENTS

11. Finding A Purpose in Life 71

12. Meeting Goals With Your Needs: the Balance Between Ambition and Well-Being 77

13. Health, Energy And Abundance 84

14. Decision Making 88

15. The Power of Letting Go and Forgiveness 94

16. The Law of Attraction- Manifesting Your Best Life 100

17. How Travel Changes Your Mindset: Travel Like A Traveler, Not A Tourist 107

18. How Food Impacts Your Thinking: the Mind-Body Connection 113

19. Gratitude As a Foundation 117

Conclusion 124

ABOUT THE AUTHOR

*D*r. Parnavi Ganatra is a passionate writer, certified life coach, and an advocate for holistic well-being. With a background in dentistry and a deep interest in personal growth, spirituality, and mindset transformation, Parnavi has dedicated her journey to helping others unlock their true potential and live fulfilling lives. Drawing wisdom from ancient philosophies, modern neuroscience, and real-life examples, she weaves powerful insights into practical lessons of everyday. Through her writing and vision, Parnavi aims to inspire people to embrace self-love, gratitude, and resilience as tools for personal transformation. The Abundance Within is her heartfelt offering as a torchbearer in guiding readers on their path towards happiness, purpose, and peace.

THE ABUNDANCE WITHIN: WEALTH, HAPPINESS AND FULFILLMENT IN EVERY ASPECT OF LIFE

INTRODUCTION

*I*n a world driven by deadlines, desires, and distractions, we often find ourselves chasing external validation—whether in the form of wealth, recognition, or happiness. But what if everything we seek already exists within us? *The Abundance Within* is not just a book; it is an invitation to pause, reflect, and rediscover the infinite potential, peace, and prosperity that reside within your mind, heart, and soul.

Everywhere we turn, we are inundated with messages about achieving success, finding happiness, and living our best lives. Yet, despite the abundance of resources—self-help guides, social media, and more—many people still feel unfulfilled, anxious, and disconnected. Why? Because true abundance is not found in external achievements but in your mindset, habits, and ability to align with the universal energy that surrounds us.

What to Expect in This Journey

The chapters ahead are thoughtfully crafted to help you understand and embrace the key principles that foster abundance in every aspect of your life— your mindset, relationships, health, finances and spiritual well-being.

You'll discover:

- The importance of cultivating a resilient and growth-oriented mindset.
- How gratitude, forgiveness and mindfulness can transform your emotional and mental landscape
- The science behind abundance- exploring neuroscience, quantum physics and universal energy
- A shift in your mindset, money and relationships
- How ancient wisdom from Hinduism, Buddhism, Christianity, Islam and other spiritual traditions align with modern psychological principles.
- Real life stories of people who overcame challenges and achieved remarkable success by tapping into their inner abundance.

The Universal Energy Within You: Your Inner Goldmine

Have you ever wondered why meeting a joyful person suddenly uplifts your spirits while meeting a negative person withdraws it? The word "vibe" is not a cliché–it's actually a term that enlightens us regarding the term "energy." At the heart of this book lies one fundamental truth: You are a powerful being connected to an infinite source of universal energy, or simply, the flow of life is always available to you. The key is to learn how to tap into it, align with it and allow it to guide your thoughts, actions and intentions.

Science now supports what ancient philosophies have long taught: Our thoughts, emotions and frequencies shape our reality. By raising your energy through gratitude, love, money mindset and positive intentions, you can attract abundance effortlessly.

Who Is This Book for?

- If you are tired of feeling stuck in cycles of limitation and lack
- If you are seeking clarity, purpose and a deeper connection with yourself
- If you are someone who believes in growth, transformation and the power of your mindset

Whether you are just starting on your journey of self discovery or you are someone who has been on this path for years, The Abundance Within offers timeless wisdom, practical strategies and gentle reminders that you already have everything you need to live a fulfilling life. This isn't just a book to read- it's a guide to experience. Each chapter will reflect and dive you within yourself.

A Personal Invitation

As the author of this book, my intention isn't just to give you all the answers, but present you with powerful tools, insights and stories that can transform your lives. This journey is not about becoming someone else, it's about becoming more of who you truly are. It's about peeling

ABOUT THE AUTHOR

away the layers of doubt, fear and societal conditioning to reveal the abundant being you have always been.

Take a deep breath. Trust this journey and most importantly, trust yourself.

Let's begin.

> *"Abundance is not something we acquire. It is something we tune into."*
>
> **– Wayne Dyer**

1

MINDSET MATTERS

"Your mindset is the lens through which you see the world. Change the lens and the world changes with it."

---

*I*t's the foundation of your beliefs, thoughts, actions and ultimately, the life you create for yourself. Everything begins in the mind-how you perceive challenges, celebrate success and define your possibilities. Whether you think you can or you can't, you are right. The simple yet profound truth underscores the power of our mindset.

What is Mindset?

Mindset refers to your collective thoughts and beliefs that shape your attitude, habits and behavior. Broadly there are two types of mindsets:

Fixed mindset: Believing that your abilities, talents, and intelligence are static and cannot be changed.

Growth Mindset: Believing that abilities can be developed through effort, learning and perseverance. As *Dr. Carol Dweck* states, "The view you adopt for yourself profoundly affects the way you lead your life."

You can either have a victory mindset or a victim mindset as mentioned by *Mr Sanjay Kathuria* in one of his talks. Your mindset determines everything. During the battlefield, *Arjuna* once said to *Lord Krishna* that he is able to control the wind, but not able to control his mind. So, it's very critical to gain an upper hand on your mind to achieve your desired results.

Kobe Bryant, an American basketball player, once said that, *"If you know what you want, the world becomes your library."* India's Prime Minister, *Narendra Modi* also said that, *"Till the time you keep your student active inside you, you will keep on progressing."*

For example, *Thomas Edison*, the man who discovered light bulb, when asked about his failures, stated that "*I have not failed. I have just found 10,000 new ways that won't work.*" Edison's ability to reframe failure into learning experience exemplifies the growth mindset.

Examples of Mindset Effect in Animals

As a young calf, an elephant is tied with heavy chains. It struggles tirelessly to break free but fails. Over time, it learns that resistance is futile. As the elephant grows, the chains are replaced with a simple rope—something it could easily break. Yet, conditioned by its past failures, it never tries, believing escape is impossible.

This illustrates a powerful truth: our mindset can be our greatest limitation or our strongest weapon. In the battle of life, success or failure often depends not on our abilities, but on what we believe to be possible.

Why Mindset Matters?

1. Shapes your reality:

Your thoughts create your world. If you approach life with negativity, you will find obstacles everywhere. But a positive outlook helps you see opportunities even during adversities.

Example: *Oprah Winfrey* faced poverty as well as abuse in her childhood. Instead of letting her circumstances define her, she adopted a mindset of resilience, becoming one of the most influential people in the world.

2. Drives Action:

A strong growth-oriented mindset pushes you to take action, even when the odds seem against you. It is the belief in possibility that catalyzes hard work and persistence.

Example: *Elon musk's* mindset to solve global challenges led him to create Tesla and SpaceX, despite initial failures and widespread skepticism.

3. Impacts emotional resilience:

Your mindset depends on how you react to failures. Do you see it as a dead end or a stepping-stone? People with a growth mindset embrace failure as a part of the process.

Mindset in Science: The Neuroplastic Brain

Modern neuroscience reveals that our brains are highly malleable and adaptable. We can actively 'rewire' our thought patterns by intentionally practising positive thinking. When you repeatedly focus on empowering thoughts, you strengthen neural pathways associated with optimism, problem-solving, and resilience. Over time, these pathways become your brain's default mode of thinking.

Negative thinking often triggers the amygdala, activating the brain's stress response. In contrast, positive reframing engages the prefrontal cortex, which helps regulate emotions and enhance problem-solving abilities.

According to research by Brazilian neuroscientist *Suzana Herculano-Houzel*, the human brain contains approximately 86 billion neurons. These neurons continuously form new neural pathways based on how you shape your mindset. However, studies suggest that in many people, very few new pathways develop over time, as their mindset remains largely unchanged. In fact, neuronal depletion is commonly observed with age.

Example: Studies show that practicing gratitude strengthens neural networks associated with optimism and well-being. Monks who practice mindfulness regularly showed an increase in the gray matter density in the prefrontal cortex(responsible for decision-making) and exhibited significantly enhanced brain plasticity, allowing them to remain calm and focused under pressure.

Experiments to prove the power of thoughts

Dr. Fabrizio Benedetti and his colleagues studied a group of patients undergoing thoracic surgery. Since it is a highly invasive procedure, morphine—a painkiller—is routinely administered post-surgery. Half of the patients received the dose from a doctor at their bedside, while the other half received the exact same dose via an IV through a pre-programmed pump.

Surprisingly, the group that received the morphine from a doctor reported significantly lower pain levels, as their awareness of the treatment appeared to enhance its effectiveness.

In another study, *Dr. Alia Crum* and her colleagues divided participants into two groups, both of whom were given the exact same milkshake. Blood samples were taken to measure ghrelin, the hormone that rises with hunger and drops after eating.

One group was told that the shake contained only 130 calories and was a healthy option. This group showed only a slight decrease in ghrelin levels. In contrast, the other group, who believed the shake contained around 630 calories, experienced a significant drop in ghrelin.

This study highlights the powerful role mindset plays in shaping our physiological responses and, ultimately, our lives.

Mindset in Ancient Teachings

Mindset has been emphasized in various religious and philosophical traditions:

In **Hinduism**, the Bhagavad Gita teaches the importance of a focused and detached mindset. Lord Krishna advises Arjuna to perform his duties without being attached to the results, emphasizing mental clarity and resilience.

In **Buddhism**, the Buddha taught us that our thoughts shape our reality: *"What we think, we become."* The practice of mindfulness, a cornerstone of Buddhism, helps cultivate awareness and positive outlook.

In **Christianity**, the Bible teaches the power of faith and positive outlook. *"Do not conform to the pattern of this world but be transformed by the renewing of your mind."*

In **Islam**, teachings like *Tawakkul, Shukr* and *Sabr* emphasis the importance of trust, gratitude and patience as a hallmark of strong mindset.

5. Neuroscience meets Spirituality

Practices like prayer, meditation and affirmations combine ancient wisdom with modern neuroscience to rewire the brain for a positive and focused mindset.

'Sankalp se srishti,' the phrase used by *Bhramakumari sister Shivani* throws light on the same essence.

Real life Stories of Mindset Transformation

Michael Jordan was rejected from his high school basketball team. He used this setback as a fuel to work harder. His growth mindset transformed him into a sports legend

J.K. Rowling faced multiple rejections for Harry Potter, but her belief in her story and persistence paid off, made her one of the most successful authors of all time.

Kapil Sharma, a renowned Indian comedian, generally asks this question to most of the celebrities on his show: *"Did you ever think you would get a chance to be at The Kapil Sharma Show?"* This might be just a form of humor, but it definitely raised his frequency and helped him in manifesting fame.

How to Cultivate a Winning Mindset

1. Reframe challenges

Instead of saying, *"This is too hard,"* ask yourself, *"What can I learn from this?"* Every challenge is a hidden opportunity for growth.

2. Practice Gratitude

Gratitude rewires your brain to focus on abundance rather than lack. Start each day by listing a few things that you are grateful for.

3. Visualize success

Visualization activates the brain's motor cortex, preparing it for actual success. Imagine yourself achieving goals daily.

4. Surround yourself with positivity

The people and environments you surround yourself with influence your mindset. Seek out relationships that inspire growth and optimism.

5. Focus on growth, not perfection

Celebrate small wins. Progress, no matter how slow, is still progress. Execution is always better than perfection.

Closing Thoughts

Your mindset is your most powerful tool. It determines whether you thrive or merely survive. By shifting your thoughts, embracing growth and failure both, believing in yourself, you can create a life of good vibes and boundless possibilities.

What's one belief holding you back today? Write it down and replace it with an empowering thought. Watch how your mindset starts to change your reality.

2

BREAKING FREE FROM LIMITING BELIEFS

"Whether you think you can, or you think you can't – you are right."
– Henry Ford

The Invisible Chains of Limiting Beliefs

Imagine standing in front of an open door, but refusing to walk through it because you believe it's locked. Limiting beliefs are like those invisible locks— they exist only in your mind but can stop you from achieving your success and happiness.

What are Limiting Beliefs?

Limiting beliefs are deeply rooted assumptions or thoughts that hold you back from reaching your potential. They often sound like:

"I'm not good enough."

"Success is only for lucky people."

"I can't change, it's just who I am."

These beliefs are not facts— they are stories you have accepted as truth.

Where do Limiting Beliefs Come From?

Understanding the source of your limiting beliefs is the first step to breaking them.

Childhood Conditioning

Statements from parents, teachers, or authority figures such as *"Money doesn't grow on trees"* or *"You will never be successful in that field"* can shape our beliefs from a young age.

Past Experiences

A past failure may have led you to believe, *"I am not capable of success."* Over time, this belief can become deeply ingrained, affecting your confidence and future decisions.

Society and Culture

Cultural narratives, stereotypes, and societal pressures can create invisible boundaries. For example, messages like *"You must always come first in class"* or *"You have to become a doctor or an engineer"* can instill limiting beliefs about success and self-worth.

Self talk

The words you repeat to yourself daily can shape your reality. Negative self-talk gradually becomes a pattern, which then subconsciously manifests in your life.

How many of you have experienced repeated breakups or constant setbacks in relationships and careers? Have you ever wondered why, despite taking action, you somehow sabotage your progress, and the pattern keeps repeating? This time, take a moment to introspect. What are your beliefs about relationships? Do you believe that *"Relationships don't last"* or something similar? Or do you feel that *"This career doesn't offer much growth"*?

Remember, our beliefs are powerful, and these patterns must be broken through conscious self-reflection and positive self-talk.

The Power of Awareness

You can't change what you are not aware of. You don't appreciate things that you don't have knowledge of. Awareness is the flashlight that reveals the shadows of your liming beliefs. So next time a limiting thought crosses your mind, pause, observe and ask whether it is true or is there any evidence supporting this belief? Most limiting beliefs fall apart when you question their validity and replace them with empowering beliefs.

The Role of Fear in Limiting Beliefs

Fear is often the root cause of limiting beliefs– fear of failure, fear of rejection and fear of success. Fear thrives in uncertainty. When you confront it, it loses its power.

The Psychology behind Limiting Beliefs

Neuroscience shows us that our brains are wired to protect us from discomfort and perceived threats. When we experience failure, rejection or trauma, our brain forms neural pathways associated with those events. These pathways can create automatic responses, leading us to avoid similar situations in the future.

The Reticular Activating System(RAS) in our brain filters information based on what we believe to be true. If you believe you are unworthy of success, your brain will provide evidence supporting your belief while ignoring evidence that contradicts it.

The good news? Neuroplasticity– our brain's ability to rewire and form new pathways– means you can replace old, limiting beliefs with empowering ones.

Spiritual Perspectives on Limiting Beliefs

In **Hinduism**, the Bhagavad Gita emphasizes *"You are what you believe yourself to be."* Krishna teaches Arjuna that your mind can be your friend or your enemy depending on how it is controlled.

In **Christianity**, the Bible says, *"As a man thinketh in his heart, so is he."* Faith and belief play a central role in overcoming internal obstacles.

In **Buddhism**, the teachings highlight, *"What you think you become. What you feel you attract. What you imagine you create."*

In **Islam** too, the Quran teaches *"Indeed, Allah will not change the condition of people until they change what is in themselves."*

From these teachings, it's clear that breaking free from limiting beliefs is both a spiritual as well as mental practice.

Exercises to vercome Limiting Beliefs

Daily affirmations, visualization and replacing your old beliefs with new empowering ones can help break them. It is mandatory to feel limitless, worthy and capable of achieving greatness.

Final Thoughts

Breaking free from limiting beliefs is not a one-time task; it's an ongoing journey. Every time you confront fear, self doubt or hesitation, remind yourself: Your beliefs are the strongest thing, more powerful than your thoughts or feelings that create your reality. You have the power to rewrite your story, change your mindset and create a life filled with purpose, abundance and joy.

3
SELF LOVE AND ACCEPTANCE

*I*n a world where comparison and criticism are constant companions, cultivating self love and acceptance feels like a radical act. Yet, it is one of the most liberating and empowering choices you can make. Self love is not selfish; it's the foundation upon which all growth, happiness and meaningful connections are built.

The foundation of self love

Self love begins with an understanding that you are inherently worthy; not because of your achievements, appearance or the validation of others, but simply because you exist. You are a unique expression of life, with qualities, quirks, and gifts that no one else has.

However, many of us grow up learning to seek approval from others, measuring our worth by external standards. This constant chase leaves us disconnected from our true selves. To love yourself means to stop seeking validation outside and start finding it within.

For example, a plant doesn't compare itself to the trees or flowers around it. It simply grows in its own time, own height, taking it what it needs from the soil and the sun. Your journey of self love is similar– you need to nurture yourself without judgment or comparison.

A story to reflect on:

There was once a young woman named *Maya* who always felt like she was not enough. No matter how hard she worked, there was always someone more smarter, prettier, or more successful. She compared her life to others and always found herself lacking.

One day, Maya visited a small pottery workshop. She watched the potter shape a lump of clay into a beautiful vase. Curious, she asked the potter, "How do you make it so perfect?"

The potter smiled and said, "It's not perfect. Look closely, and you will see tiny cracks and uneven curves. But that's what makes it unique. If I tried to make it flawless, I'd take away its character. The beauty lies in the imperfections and flaws."

Maya realized something that day: she had been chasing perfection, not realizing that her flaws and imperfections were part of what made her unique. Like the vase, she was beautiful because of her cracks, not in spite of them.

An Enlightenment:

Imagine you have a five-year-old child who accidentally loses something precious of yours. How long would you stay upset or angry—an hour or two at most? Then why are you so harsh on yourself when you make a mistake? Don't you value yourself just as much as you value that child?

Now, think about this: if someone says something hurtful to you, how long do you hold onto it? Probably for years. That person may have forgotten their words, yet you continue to punish yourself over and over. It's natural to feel hurt, but it is not necessary to let that pain linger in your mind indefinitely.

Let go. You deserve the same kindness and forgiveness that you offer to others.

Steps to Cultivate Self-Love

1. Accept your imperfections:

Perfection is an illusion. Embrace your flaws—they make you human and relatable. A cracked vase can still hold water; in fact, its imperfections can make it unique. The first step towards self-love is trusting yourself, acknowledging your emotions, believing in your worth, and challenging your inner critic.

2. Avoid labels:

In the process of criticizing yourself you give a lot of labels to yourself either by your own beliefs or external people. Avoid these labels and start accepting and embracing your own worth and unique self.

3. Set boundaries:

Loving yourself means valuing your time, energy, space and mental health. Learn to say No without guilt and with compassion. Be assertive. Boundaries are not walls to keep people out but lines that define how you deserve to be treated.

4. Celebrate your wins:

Big or small, every step forward is a victory. Celebrate yourself even for the things you take for granted- getting through a tough day, being kind to someone or simply showing up.

5. Treat yourself with compassion:

When you make mistakes or face setbacks, resist the urge to criticize yourself harshly. Speak to yourself as you would to a dear friend. Compassion is a bridge to healing and growth. Try to keep your self esteem higher than anything. Do not be a people pleaser.

Role of Acceptance in Self Love

Acceptance is the gateway to self-love. It means acknowledging where you are in life without resistance or judgment. However, acceptance doesn't mean giving up on growth; rather, it fosters the clarity and peace needed to move forward.

For example, when a river encounters rocks, it doesn't stop or try to force its way through. Instead, it flows around them, continuing its journey. Similarly, accepting yourself as you are today allows you to navigate life's obstacles with grace.

Accepting Yourself with Reflection

The quality of your relationships with others depends on the relationship you have with yourself. Consider the world as a mirror, reflecting who you are. If you look in a mirror and like what you see, you smile. But if you dislike your reflection, you might frown or make faces—not because the mirror is flawed, but because it simply reflects your perception of yourself.

For instance, if you dislike your eyebrows, you'll frown at your reflection. But if you appreciate them, you'll smile. Similarly, the world acts as a mirror, reflecting your inner self through external experiences—whether in the form of criticism, harsh words, or challenges. The key is that if you fully accept yourself, you won't be easily affected by the judgments or actions of others.

If something triggers you, it often points to an unresolved wound or a part of yourself you're judging. The choice is yours: either embrace and love yourself as you are or make changes for your own growth and betterment. The ultimate formula is to be comfortable with who you are.

Break those Limiting Rules

All of us have preset rules in our minds that become the root cause of our emotional triggers. For example, if someone shouts at you, you might feel humiliated because you associate shouting with disrespect. But what if you shift your mindset and no longer equate shouting with disrespect? In that case, shouting would no longer trigger you, and feelings of humiliation would no longer take root. This doesn't mean that shouting is acceptable—it simply means that it will no longer have the power to affect your peace of mind.

Real Life Examples

Lizzo, the singer, rapper, and body positivity advocate *Lizzo* is a shining example of self-love in action. Despite facing criticism and societal pressure to conform to unrealistic beauty standards, she continues to celebrate her individuality and encourages others to do the same.

Lizzo's journey proves that self-love isn't about fitting in—it's about embracing your authentic self.

Michelle Obama, Former First Lady of the United States, *Michelle Obama,* has openly spoken about experiencing *imposter syndrome*—the feeling of not being good enough or not belonging. Through her speeches, interviews, and memoir, she beautifully shares her journey of self-love, self-acceptance, and personal growth, inspiring countless others to embrace their worth.

Challenges to Self Love and How to Overcome them

1. Comparison Culture:

Social media can make it easy to compare your life to the reel life of others. Remember, people always share their best moments, not their struggles. You need to remind yourself that everyone's journey is different.

2. Negative self-talk:

The voice in your head can be your biggest critic. Challenge these thoughts by asking, *"Is this thought true, or am I just being too harsh on myself?"* Replace negative statements like, *"I am not good enough"* or *"Why is this happening to me?"* with affirmations such as, *"I am learning and growing from this"* or *"I am so blessed to have gained a lesson from this."*

3. Seeking external validation:

Understand that the opinion of others doesn't define your worth. True validation comes from within. Note what you love about yourself without seeking external validation.

Science behind Practicing Self-Love:

Practicing self-love activates your brain's prefrontal cortex and releases dopamine, the "feel-good" hormone, which rewires the brain to focus on positivity, building a stronger foundation for self-acceptance. Moreover, the brain's default mode network, responsible for self-reflection, becomes overactive with negative self-talk. However, self-love helps calm it down, fostering self-compassion.

Self-Love in Religious and Spiritual Teachings:

The concept of *Aham Brahmasmi* ("I am divine") from the **Upanishads** teaches, *"I am infinite, eternal, and complete."* This wisdom reminds us that self-love is not ego but a recognition of our divine nature and inherent wholeness.

Buddhism emphasizes *metta*, or unconditional love and kindness toward oneself. The Buddha taught that self-compassion is the first step towards extending love to others. *Metta Bhavana* meditation includes affirmations such as, *"May I be happy, may I be healthy, may I live with ease."*

The *Dalai Lama* speaks of self-love as the foundation of self-compassion. Without accepting and loving ourselves, we cannot truly love others.

Christianity teaches self-love as implicit in the commandment, *"Love your neighbor as yourself."* This assumes that self-love is essential to loving others.

Mother Teresa's compassion stemmed from her deep faith in God and her understanding of her own worth as his creation. She believed that caring for oneself enabled her to care for others.

In **Islam**, the *nafs* (self) is a creation of Allah, deserving care and respect. The Quran states, *"And We have certainly honored the children of Adam."* This affirms that every individual is inherently worthy.

The principle of *Ahimsa* in **Jainism** extends to oneself as well. True self-love means avoiding harm—both physical and emotional—and treating oneself with gentleness.

The Ripple Effect of Self-Love

When you love and accept yourself, you radiate that energy to the world. You inspire others to do the same thing, creating a ripple effect of positivity and empowerment. Self-love is not just a gift to yourself; it's a gift to everyone around you.

Self-love and acceptance are not destinations to reach, but a journey. They require patience, practice and a commitment to treat yourself with kindness and respect. As you embark on this path, remember that you are also worthy of all the love you give to others.

Action step:

Take a moment right now to say aloud, "*I love and accept myself exactly the way I am.*" Feel the power of those words and let them guide you towards a more powerful and fulfilling life.

4
THE POWER OF RELATIONSHIPS

Relationships are the threads that weave the fabric in our lives. They shape our experiences, influence our perspective and determine the quality of our emotional and mental well-being. Whether it's our relationship with family, friends, romantic partners, colleagues or relationship with ourselves, each connection carries the power to heal, inspire and transform us.Relationships are the single most powerful force in our lives that shape our daily lives in countless ways. Relationships have a profound impact on our mindset, personal growth and overall happiness. Healthy relationships can serve as a foundation for success and fulfillment, while also addressing how to set boundaries and let go of toxic connections.

The real meaning of relationships is relating with each other. Co-regulation is much better than self-regulation even if it is a sign of independence. One shows that if you stand in front of the hill alone, your body will perceive the height of the hill higher than if you were to stand in front of a hill with a friend.

If I were to ask you what is the most single important best time in your life, if you reflect on it relationships would always be a part of it and if it weren't then the first thing you would want to do after a most amazing experience would share about it to someone.

The Science behind Relationships and Well-being

Science shows that if you want to live a happy, healthy, and fulfilling life, the most important factor is having strong connections and friendships. Yet, we often dismiss and sideline this crucial aspect of our well-being.

Did you know that having close relationships makes you less likely to catch a cold and helps you recover faster from surgery? In fact, strong social connections can reduce the risk of major health challenges by two to five times.

Neuroscience reveals that human connection is not just a luxury—it's a biological necessity. Studies show that positive relationships release oxytocin, a hormone that reduces stress, boosts mood, and fosters trust.

Studies showing the Significance of Relationships

According to *Harvard's* study of Adult Development, one of the longest studies on happiness, the key to a fulfilling life isn't wealth or fame- it's actually strong and meaningful relationships.

A study at *Brigham Young university* found this that if you have deep and strong relationships you will live longer than the other people. Not having good relationships is equivalent to smoking 15 cigarettes a day.

Social psychologists at *Harvard* found that the friendships account to 90 percent of your success or failure in life.

In a recent statement given by *Marc Randolph*, the CEO of Netflix, mentioned that he has a Tuesday date night tradition with his wife that helped him maintain work-life balance. He would leave work by 5pm on Tuesdays to spend time with his wife which kept him sane and put the rest of his work in right perspective.

Universal Energy and the Relationships

Everything in the universe, whether living or non-living, is made up of energy. At the energy level, all are one. We are all connected, forming a unified field of existence. When you begin to love and accept others as they are, you naturally form deeper connections with them.

It's important to recognize that everyone shares the same fundamental fears, doubts, excitement, and emotions. If you dislike something about a person or wish to change them, the first step is to accept and love them as they are. Then, work on healing or changing that aspect within yourself and start speaking positively about it. Since energy is interconnected, your internal shift will naturally influence the other person as well.

The Root of All Relationships – Your Parents

Just as seeds cannot grow without a strong connection to the earth, children who lack a healthy relationship with their parents often struggle to flourish in other relationships.

From the moment you are born, your subconscious mind begins forming relationship patterns based on your connection with your parents. It has been observed that the nature of your relationship with them often manifests in your interactions with others—whether with colleagues, friends, or romantic partners. You attract people and experiences that align with your internal frequency and patterns. Interestingly, the traits you may struggle with in your parents often resurface in your bosses or partners, reflecting unresolved dynamics within you.

Healthy Relationships Are Rooted in Authenticity

When you show up as your true self—vulnerable, honest, and without pretense—you create space for others to do the same. According to *Sue Johnson*, a relationship expert, the markers of secure relationships are accessibility, responsiveness, and emotional engagement.

Jen Michel Pollock says, "Our connections have grown broader, but shallower."

What is Infatuation?

It is nothing but seeing too many positives and ignoring the negatives of a person, job, goal, or anything, while hatred is when you see many negatives and fewer positives. This causes an imbalanced perspective, leading to connections that might not serve you or your purpose. An imbalanced perspective is an addiction and can consume your whole day in memories. Thus, it is of utmost importance to view everything with a holistic approach.

Moreover, qualities such as listening, smiling, politeness, helping, complimenting, punctuality, and apologizing can win a person's trust and help build an authentic connection.

So how do we actually build much deeper and more meaningful relationships?

Self-acceptance first:

The relationship you have with yourself and your parents, as they are the first relation you develop in your lives, sets the tone of every other connection in your life.

Active listening:

True connection requires being fully present in conversations, without distractions or judgment.

For example, *Oprah Winfrey* often credits her close friendship with Maya Angelou for being the source of strength and guidance. Their bond was built on trust, mutual respect, honesty and emotional vulnerability.

The Role of Relationships in Personal Growth

Every relation serves a purpose— some are meant to teach, some to heal, and others to inspire.

Relationships as mirrors:

People around us often reflect on our strengths, weaknesses and unresolved issues.

Support system:

Having people who uplift, motivate and support you during your tough times can make a lot of difference.

For example, *Nelson Mandela's* relationship with his friend and fellow activist, *Oliver Tambo*, played a crucial role in his resilience and leadership. Their mutual trust and shared vision kept their spirits alive during the darkest times of apartheid.

Managing Conflicts

There is no such thing as a perfect relationship with anyone. To manage conflicts, you need to ask yourself: *What is more important at this moment—your goal or your relationship?* You can choose to be aggressive, take control of the situation, and win your goal; you can be submissive and prioritize your relationship; or you can be passive and avoid the situation altogether. However, the ideal approach is to be assertive—a skill you need to develop—by staying calm and communicating openly.

Some Key Differences between Men and Women

Understanding the fundamental differences between men and women can help resolve many conflicts. Studies suggest that, apart from biological and hormonal differences, their brains are also wired differently. Men's brains have more grey matter (processing power), while women's brains tend to have more white matter (connecting power).

Metaphorically, it is said that a man's brain has compartments or "rooms" for different things that are not connected to each other, whereas a woman's brain has interconnected "rooms," allowing her to link everything together. This is why women tend to recall details that men often forget. Interestingly, men have something called a *"nothing zone,"* where they simply want to do nothing for a while—one reason why they often take longer in the bathroom or enjoy activities like fishing.

Men typically focus on task-driven, solution-oriented approaches, while women are more likely to consider emotional and relational dynamics. When women share their thoughts, it is often an emotional release rather than a request for a solution. She may not even mean everything she says at that moment. The problem arises when men, who are solution-focused, try to offer fixes immediately. Women don't need solutions right away—maybe later—but in that moment, they just need to be heard.

The communication styles of men and women also differ. Men are brief talkers who focus on exchanging information, whereas women prefer to express themselves in detail. Proper communication and acknowledging these differences can help cultivate better, more understanding relationships.

Religious and Spiritual Teachings on Relationships

In **Hinduism**, relationships are seen as karmic bonds-each person in your life is there for a reason, either to teach you a lesson or help you grow. Hence, treat every relationship with respect and gratitude.

The **Bible** too, emphasizes love as the core of human connection. In John 15:12, the Bible says, *"Love each other as I have loved you."*

Islam too emphasizes the importance of kindness, forgiveness and trust in relationships.

Toxic Relationships and Boundaries

Not all relationships are meant to last, and not all connections are healthy. Recognizing toxic patterns is essential to maintain your emotional and mental well being.

Red flags

Constant criticism, manipulation, lack of respect, and emotional abuse are major red flags in any relationship.

The Power of Saying No

Setting boundaries isn't selfish; it is necessary. It reflects the beauty of Yang energy within each of us. If someone has a habit of being controlling, and their need for control is excessive, it can negatively affect you. However, the real issue is not their controlling nature but your inability to assertively say *no*.

Moreover, it is important to recognize that you cannot change everyone. The mindset of *"Let them"* is crucial—allowing people to be who they are rather than trying to change or control them. Attempting to do so often leads to unnecessary conflict and emotional strain.

For example, actress and mental health advocate *Selena Gomez* has openly discussed the importance of letting go of toxic relationships. She emphasized that stepping away from harmful connections was essential for her healing and personal growth.

Practical Steps to Strengthen Relationships

1. **Communicate openly**
   Honest conversations build trust and reduce misunderstandings.
2. **Show appreciation**
   Regularly express gratitude for the people in your life.
3. **Spend quality time**
   Create moments of connection without distractions.
4. **Forgive and let go**
   Holding onto grudges only harms you in the long run. Do you know when someone's attitude is at its peak? It's when they say, *"I forgive you."*
5. **Check-in regularly**
   Ask people how they are truly feeling and be present for them.

Connection is the Key

Relationships are not just about sharing time– they are about sharing energy, emotions and experiences. The power of relationships lies in the ability to uplift, heal and transform. Whether it's the bond with a friend, a family member, or even yourself, every relation has the potential to shape your journey.

> *"Surround yourself with people who inspire you, challenge you and bring out the best in you."*

5

THE BEAUTIFUL BALANCE OF YIN AND YANG: MASCULINE AND FEMININE ENERGY

At the core of a harmonious and fulfilling life lies the delicate balance between two fundamental energies: The masculine (Yang) and feminine (Yin). These energies are not defined by gender but are universal forces present in every individual, shaping our emotions, actions and relationships.

In ancient philosophies like **Taoism** and spiritual traditions such as **Hinduism**, these energies are symbolized as Yin and Yang in Taoist thought and as *Shiva* and *Shakti* in Hindu philosophy. When these energies are balanced, they create harmony within individuals as well as the world around us.

Understanding Yin and Yang Energy

Yin (Feminine energy):

Represents stillness, intuition, receptivity, compassion, vulnerability, and emotional depth. It is the energy of the moon, night, and water—calm, flowing, and nurturing.

Yang (Masculine energy):

Represents action, strength, structure, focus, and logic. It is the energy of the sun, day, and fire—dynamic, bold, and goal-oriented.

Neither is superior to the other; instead, they complement and complete each other. Just as night balances day, the interplay of these energies creates a holistic and fulfilling life. A balance of both energies is essential for every individual, regardless of gender.

Shiva and Shakti: The Divine Union

In Hindu philosophy, Shiva represents pure consciousness (masculine energy), while Shakti represents creative energy (feminine energy)—vibrant and full of movement.

Shiva without Shakti: Pure potential without action.

Shakti without Shiva: Endless energy without direction.

Together, they symbolize the union of power and purpose, creation and consciousness. In the *Ardhanarishvara* form, they merge into one divine being, illustrating a perfect balance of masculine and feminine energy in every individual.

Balance in Daily Life

In our daily lives, the interplay of these energies reflects in our choices, behaviors and relationships as well.

When Masculine Energy Dominates(Yang dominance)

Overworking, burnout, aggressiveness, rigidity, excessive logic, need for control, and emotional detachment.

When Feminine Energy Dominates (Yin dominance)

Lack of structure, indecisiveness, over-dependency, inability to say no, and emotional overwhelm.

Achieving Balance:

An imbalance of energies can create a rift within oneself and also within relationships. Accepting the dominant traits of others can help inculcating those traits (energy) within you and help achieve balance. When you need clarity and focus tap into masculine energy. When you need introspection and creativity tap into feminine energy.

For example, in business, masculine energy helps in strategic planning, decision making and goal orientation, while feminine energy aids in creativeness, collaboration and emotional intelligence to the table. A successful leader will always blend both of these seamlessly to reach heights.

Real Life example of Balanced Energy

Indira Nooyi, former CEO of PepsiCo, is an excellent example of balancing masculine and feminine energies. Her masculine(Yang) allows her to make bold decisions, lead with a practical mindset and handle corporate challenges, while her feminine energies enable her to lead with empathy, nurture her team and cultivate meaningful connections. Together, these energies create a leadership style that inspires millions.

Neuroscience and the Masculine- Feminine Balance

Modern neuroscience supports the idea that balancing masculine and feminine energies can improve emotional resilience and mental well-being.

Left brain (Yang energy)

Logical reasoning, analytical thinking and problem solving.

Right brain(Yin energy)

Creativity, intuition and emotional intelligence.

Integrating both hemispheres of the brain through mindfulness, meditation and emotional awareness can create balanced mindset and reduce stress.

Religious and Spiritual Teachings on Balance

Hinduism throws light on the union of Shiva and Shakti which teaches that harmony comes from merging the physical (Shakti) with the spiritual (Shiva)

In **Buddhism**, the *Middle way* emphasizes balance– neither excessive indulgence nor extreme austerity.

Practices to Balance Yin and Yang Energies

Meditation

Calm the mind and align your inner energies.

Mindful action

Balance periods of work with rest and reflection.

Physical activities

Activities like Yoga help balance masculine and feminine flows.

Journaling

Explore your emotions(Yin) and set goals and targets (Yang).

Self-reflection

Assess your dominant energy in challenging situations.

The Gift of Balance: A Beautiful Life

When you align your masculine and feminine energies, life flows effortlessly. In relationships, you communicate with clarity and empathy. At work, you act with focus and creativity. In self care, you balance discipline with kindness towards yourself. Embracing both masculine and feminine energies makes you strong, creative, focused and intuitive.

The dance of Yin and Yang, Shiva and Shakti, creates not just a balanced individual but a balanced world. True happiness, success and inner peace arrive when these energies flow in harmony within you.

6

OVERCOMING CHALLENGES WITH GRACE

> "The greatest glory in living lies not in never falling, but in rising every time we fall."
> – Nelson Mandela

Introduction: Challenges as Opportunities for Growth

Life is a series of peaks and valleys. While the peaks fill you with joy and triumph, the valleys often test your strength, patience and resilience. Challenges are inevitable, but how you respond to them defines your character and shapes your journey.

Imagine two people facing the same obstacle- one spirals into frustration and self-pity, while the other takes a deep breath, adapts and finds a solution. So, what makes the difference? Mindset, emotional resilience and the ability to approach challenges with grace.

The Psychology of Resilience: How the Brain Handles Challenges

When we face hindrances, the brain triggers the fight-or-flight response. While this was useful for our ancestors facing physical danger, modern challenges often require thoughtful responses rather than impulsive reactions.

Neuroscience shows that the brain can adapt and rewire itself through neuroplasticity. Every time you face a challenge and respond calmly and strategically, you strengthen neural pathways that improve your ability to handle stress in the future.

Spiritual Insights on Overcoming Challenges

In the **Bhagavad Gita,** Lord Krishna advises Arjuna that, "*You have the right to perform your duty, but not to the fruits of your actions.*" This teaches you detachment from the outcomes– focusing on doing your best without being paralyzed by fear and failure.

The **Bible** reminds you that, *"Consider it pure joy when you face trials, because you know that the testing of your faith produces perseverance."* Challenges build character, patience and faith.

Buddhism philosophy emphasizes *equanimity*– a calm and balanced mind in both joy and sorrow. Challenges are seen as opportunities to practice mindfulness and self awareness.

In the **Quran**, it is written, *"Indeed, with hardships comes ease."* This profound verse teaches us that every challenge carries the seed of solution and growth.

Real-Life Stories of Triumph Over Challenges

Malala Yousafzai survived an assassination attempt for advocating girls' education. Instead of letting fear stop her, she rose with courage, became a global icon, and won the Nobel Peace Prize at just seventeen.

Nick Vujicic, born without arms and legs, faced immense challenges. Today, he is a world-renowned motivational speaker, spreading messages of hope and resilience.

Deepinder Goyal (CEO of Zomato) and *Ritesh Agarwal* (CEO of OYO) exemplify resilience, innovation, and unwavering belief. Their persistence during the pandemic helped them build successful businesses despite adversity.

These stories highlight a key lesson: The ability to rise after every fall is what defines true strength.

Practical Strategies of Overcoming Challenges with Grace

Shift your perspective

See challenges as opportunities for growth rather than setbacks. Ask yourself, *"What can I learn from the situation?"*

Practice mindfulness and deep breathing

When emotions run high, take a few breaths to calm your nervous system. Mindfulness helps you to stay present and respond thoughtfully.

Break it Down

Large challenges often feel overwhelming. Break them into smaller manageable steps. Celebrate small victories along the way.

Build emotional resilience

Journaling your thoughts and feelings helps process thoughts constructively. Remind yourself of past challenges you have overcome successfully.

Ask for help

Strength doesn't mean doing everything alone. Reach out to mentors, friends and professionals whenever needed.

Practice gratitude

Even in difficult times focus on small things you are grateful for. Gratitude shifts your perspective and uplifts your energy.

Emotional Intelligence: The Key to Grace Under Pressure

Emotional intelligence (EQ) is the ability to understand, manage and regulate your emotions while navigating challenging situations. Self awareness, self regulation, empathy and motivation are the core elements to recognize your triggers and emotional pattern, stay calm and composed, understand other's perspectives and keep your goals in sight despite setbacks.

Grace is a choice, not a trait. Overcoming challenges with grace doesn't mean never feeling fear, doubt or frustration. It means choosing to face these emotions, process them and respond with courage and wisdom.

You are stronger than your struggles, wiser than your worries and braver than your fears.

When life presents obstacles, meet them not with resistance but with acceptance, not with fear but with faith.

> *"You are not the drop in the ocean. You are the entire ocean in a drop."*
>
> **– Rumi**

7

LEADERSHIP MINDSET- AWAKEN THE LEADER WITHIN YOU

> "A leader is the one who knows the way, goes the way and shows the way."
> – John C. Maxwell

Leadership Is Not a title, It's a Mindset

When you hear the word leader, you often think of CEO's, presidents or some historical figures. But leadership isn't related to titles, positions or power. At its core, leadership is a mindset- a way of thinking, acting and influencing those around you.

Every person has the potential to be a leader, whether it's in their family, workplace or community. The real question is: *Are you ready to awaken the leader within you?*

Understanding the Leadership Mindset

A leadership mindset goes beyond authority– it's about taking responsibility, inspiring others and making a positive impact. In simple words, it is about leading yourself first before you lead others.

Core Traits of a Leadership Mindset

Vision

Leaders have a clear direction and inspire others to follow.

Resilience

They face challenges head-on and bounce back stronger.

Accountability

They take ownership of both success and failure.

Empathy and Humility

They understand and value other's emotions and perspectives.

Courage

They are unafraid to make tough decisions and stand by their values.

A Few Real-Life Examples

Mahatma Gandhi had no formal authority, but led an entire nation towards independence with his vision, resilience and non-violent approach.

Satya Nadella(CEO of Microsoft) transformed Microsoft by fostering a culture of empathy, learning and innovation.

Barack Obama throughout his presidency, maintained calmness and resilience even during the most challenging times.

The Neuroscience of Leadership

Great leaders excel in three areas:

- **Self-Awareness (Prefrontal Cortex)** – Leaders understand their strengths, weaknesses, and triggers.
- **Emotional Regulation (Amygdala, located in the medial temporal lobe)** – They can manage stress and make rational decisions under pressure.
- **Empathy (Mirror Neurons)** – They connect with others, build trust, and foster collaboration.

Leadership skills can be developed over time. Through neuroplasticity, the brain can create new neural pathways, making individuals more resilient, empathetic, and strategic thinkers.

Spiritual and Religious Perspective on Leadership

In **Hinduism**, Lord Krishna's guidance to Arjuna on the battlefield highlights duty *(Dharma)*, selflessness and courage.

Christianity throws light on *Servant Leadership*. Jesus Christ exemplified *servant leadership* by prioritizing humility, compassion and service to others. He said, *"Whoever wants to be a leader among you must be your servant."*

Buddhism emphasizes on *Mindful Leadership*. They talk about awareness, equanimity and compassion. A mindful leader remains present, listens deeply and acts with clarity.

In **Islam**, leadership is seen as trust(Amanah) for God. A leader is accountable for their actions and must act with justice and integrity.

"Everyone of you is a Shepherd, and everyone of you will be asked about his flock.", Prophet Muhammad

Practical Steps to Cultivate Leadership Mindset

Lead yourself first

Build self discipline and develop good habits. Set clear goals and hold yourself accountable.

Develop emotional intelligence

Be aware of your emotions and manage them effectively. Show empathy towards others.

Communicate effectively

Be clear, confident and concise in your words. Listen actively and make others feel valued.

Embrace challenges as opportunities

See failures as lessons for growth. Stay resilient in the face of adversity.

Inspire and empower others

Recognize and celebrate other's strengths. Create an environment where people feel safe to express themselves.

The Role of Mindset in Leadership Success(Carol Dweck's Theory)

Fixed mindset believes that leadership is an innate, there; whilst growth mindset sees leadership as a skill that can be cultivated through experience and learning. Great leaders are always adaptable and open to feedback.

Every leader faces criticism, failure and self-doubt. The key is to stay calm and composed under pressure, take responsibility for mistakes and keep your vision clear and unwavering.

Leadership is a Lifelong Journey

Being a leader doesn't mean being perfect; in fact, it means being willing to grow, adapt and serve. Whether you are leading a team, your family or just yourself, remember:

"Leadership isn't about being in charge. It's about taking care of those in charge."-Simon Sinek

The world needs more leaders who lead with empathy, humility, resilience and integrity. You have a leader within you-it's time to awaken that power and make a difference.

8
FINANCIAL WELLNESS AND ABUNDANCE MINDSET

> "The real measure of your wealth would be how much you would be worth if you lost all your money."
>
> – **Anonymous**

Redefining Wealth

In today's society, wealth is often associated with monetary abundance- bank balance, investments and material possessions. Nevertheless, true financial wellness encompasses more than just accumulating wealth; it revolves around cultivating a healthy relationship with money, understanding its role in our lives and fostering a mindset that attracts abundance.

Financial wellness refers to the state of being in control of your finances, having the capacity to absorb financial shocks, being in track to meet your financial goals, and possessing the freedom to make choices that allow you to enjoy life which involves financial literacy meaning understanding financial principles and concepts, such as budgeting, saving investing and debt management; financial behavior involving implementing healthy financial habits like regular saving, prudent spending and wise investing and the last financial attitude which encompasses developing a positive and proactive approach towards managing money.

Achieving financial wellness reduces stress, enhances security and provides the freedom to pursue happiness, your passions without being constraint by financial limitations.

Scarcity vs. Abundance Mindset

Our mindset significantly influences our financial health. Two predominant mindset that shapes our relationship with money are:

Scarcity Mindset

This mindset is characterized by the belief that resources are limited. Individuals with scarcity mindset often focus on what they lack, leading to fear based financial decisions and missed opportunities.

Abundance Mindset

Coined by *Stephen Convey* in "The 7 Habits of Highly Effective People," an abundance mindset is the belief that there are enough resources and success to share with people. Those with this mindset focus on possibilities, embrace change and make decisions based on potential growth and opportunities.

Real-Life Examples

Sarah Blakely, the founder of Spanx, started her company with $5000 in savings. Despite numerous rejections, her abundance mindset and belief in endless possibilities propelled her to build a billion-dollar enterprise.

The Neuroscience of Abundance Mindset

An abundance mindset stimulates the brain's reward and motivation centers. These regions are associated with goal directed behavior, empathy and flexible thinking. When the brain perceives abundance, it releases dopamine and other neurotransmitters that promote feelings of optimism and creativity.

Research shows that adopting an abundance mindset can improve cognitive functions, such as problem solving and decision making, by reducing stress and promoting a positive outlook.

Spiritual Perspectives on Financial Abundance

Many spiritual traditions offer insights into the relationship between wealth and wealth being.

Hinduism emphasizes the concept of *Artha*, one of the four aims of human life, which refers to pursuit of wealth and prosperity through righteous ways. It teaches that wealth should be acquired ethically and used for the betterment of society.

Buddhism advocates for a balanced view of wealth, encouraging generosity *(Dana)* and detachment from material possession to achieve spiritual liberation.

Islam encourages the lawful acquisition of wealth and mandates *Zakat* (charitable giving) as a means to purify wealth and support those in need.

These perspectives highlight that financial abundance, when approached with the right intention, aligns with spiritual growth and ethical living.

A millionaire or someone with a wealth mindset has different emotions, beliefs, thoughts, and actions regarding money compared to an average person. A millionaire sees everyone as equal because, at the energy level, all are one. They believe in collective growth—when one person grows, everyone benefits. They never criticize others, even if they don't receive support. They trust themselves and others when it comes to investing and spending money.

They always express gratitude and appreciation for any amount of money, whether big or small, and have the confidence to say no without guilt.

Poverty should be seen as a feeling, not a situation. When you appreciate small amounts of money, you attract larger wealth. It is also crucial to embrace duality—just as love comes with both appreciation and criticism, financial success comes with both gains and losses. If you are unwilling to accept setbacks, you cannot grow. For example, to succeed on YouTube, you must accept both positive and negative comments; otherwise, fear of criticism will stop you from posting, and you'll miss out on great opportunities.

Most importantly, adopt a **win-win mindset**—make money in a way that benefits both you and others. If your gain comes at someone else's loss, you might profit temporarily, but at the energy level, such negativity lowers your frequency and blocks future success.

Additionally, to earn more, **invest more**. Keep in mind that **profit is a choice, while loss is a reality**.

Believe in **unconditional giving**—when you give energy in the form of money, it returns to you. Never bargain with someone poor; the blessings and goodwill you receive from them have a higher frequency than the small amount of money saved. These blessings elevate your vibration, indirectly attracting more wealth.

Finally, **love your work**, whatever it may be. Gradually expand your earning and spending comfort zone. True financial success comes when you feel comfortable and confident in the work you do.

Learn the Language of Investments

It is essential to fall in love with numbers. Treat your money as you would your own child. Whenever you invest, give your money a purpose—decide what you will do once you earn it. The teachings of Warren Buffett, *"When people are afraid, you should be greedy,"* and Tony Robbins, *"Calm, compound, and unshakeable,"* offer valuable insights into developing the right investment mindset.

What is Called to be Truly Financially Free/ Retired?

Let me ask you a question: When will you feel that you are financially free? Most people respond with answers like *"when I retire," "when I settle my children,"* or *"when I get my daughter married."* But that's not the true definition of financial freedom.

Real financial freedom is **when you stop compromising today to create an imaginary perfect tomorrow** and instead focus on making the present complete and fulfilling. It's about being able to enjoy everyday experiences without waiting for a distant milestone to feel secure.

Imagine working tirelessly, sacrificing your present like a slave, just to achieve a major goal like funding your child's wedding. This doesn't mean such goals are unimportant; it simply means that the feeling of financial freedom should come from within—when you can comfortably afford small joys like dining out twice a month, visiting a salon, or watching a movie every fortnight.

These experiences vary for each individual, but the moment you start feeling financially free in your daily life, you naturally cultivate an abundance mindset, which ultimately helps you achieve even more.

Cultivating an Abundance Mindset

Shifting from scarcity to abundance mindset requires intentional effort and practice.

Practicing Gratitude

Regularly acknowledging and appreciating what you have shifts your focus from lack to abundance. Gratitude fosters positivity and opens the mind to new opportunities.

Set clear financial goals

Define what financial success looks like for you. Is it the big things which you spent on once in a blue moon for which you toil and starve every single day or the daily small experiences which makes you financially free. Clear goals provide direction and motivation, transforming abstract desires into actionable plans.

Invest in Yourself

Allocate resources for your personal and professional development. Education, skill training and health are investments that yield long term results.

Surround yourself with positivity

Engage with individuals who exhibit a positive relationship with money and support your financial aspirations. A supportive environment encourages growth and reinforces an abundance mindset.

Give back

Sharing resources, whether through charity, mentorship, giving value or community development, reinforces the belief in abundance and creates a cycle of positivity and generosity.

Overcoming Financial Challenges

Financial challenges are inevitable, but an abundance mindset equips you navigate it through with grace. View financial setbacks as learning opportunities rather than failures. This perspective fosters resilience and continuous improvement.

Maintaining ethical standards is mandatory. Uphold integrity in all financial dealings. Ethical behaviors build trust and long-term success.

Recognize that true abundance involves both material prosperity and spiritual fulfillment. Strive for harmony between the two.

Embracing Financial Wellness and Abundance

Financial wellness is not merely about accumulating wealth but a balanced healthy relationship with money. By cultivating an abundance mindset, you align your financial practices with both neurological well being and spiritual principles, paving the way for prosperous and fulfilling life.

Remember, true wealth is measured not by abundance of possessions, but by the richness of experiences, relationships and inner peace.

9
WHAT IF MONEY WAS A PERSON?

*I*magine for a moment that money isn't just paper, numbers on a screen or shiny coins, but someone you could meet, talk to and build a relationship with. What would they look like? How would they behave? More importantly, how would you behave around them?

Would you welcome them with open arms, or would you keep them at a distance? Would you trust them, or would you view them with suspicion and fear?

This perspective isn't just a playful metaphor; it's a powerful mindset shift that can change the way you attract, earn and manage wealth.

The Relationship You Have with Money

Think about your current relationship with money. If money were a person:

Are you kind and respectful to them?

Do you avoid them or chase them desperately?

Do you trust them to show up when you need them?

If your relationship with money were a romantic one, would it be healthy, balanced, and respectful? or would it be toxic, filled with mistrust and anxiety?

For example, imagine someone constantly saying, "*I hate you, but I need you.*" That's how many people feel about money these days. They desire it but resent it at the same time.

Money As a Friend or Partner

If money were a close friend or life partner:

Would you take care of them?

Would you respect their value?

Would you invest time in understanding them?

The key to financial abundance is to treat money like a trusted friend—one that supports your dreams and goals.

For example, imagine money as a person visiting your home for dinner along with another human friend. If you say, *"Oh, I didn't prepare this dinner for money—money isn't important; I did it just for you,"* how do you think your friend (money, in human form) would feel?

Now, think about this: Do you ever feel bad when your mother shows love to your friend? Probably not, because you respect both your mother and your friend. Then why do some people feel bad when someone else earns more money? If you truly love and respect money as an energy, you should feel happy when others attract it—it shows that you honor and value it, just as you would a cherished relationship.

Understanding Money's Energy

In both spiritual teachings and modern science, money is seen as energy in motion. It flows to those who are open to receiving it and repels those who fear or misuse it.

Spiritual Teachings

In **Hinduism**, *Lakshmi* represents wealth and abundance. It is taught that respecting and honoring *Lakshmi* invites more financial prosperity in life. This indicates that sending positive energy helps to attract money.

For example, *Warren Buffet* teats money not just as wealth but as a tool to create value. His relationship with money is built on respect, responsibility and long-term vision.

Breaking Negative Beliefs about Money

Many of us have grown up with negative beliefs about money:

"Money is the root of all evil."

"Rich people are greedy."

"Making money is difficult."

"Situations and people in life do not support in money making."

"I'm not good with money."

Such beliefs create a mental and emotional block. So, release all negative beliefs and be open to receiving financial abundance.

Money and Self worth

Your self-worth directly affects your net worth. If you don't believe you deserve financial abundance, it will always feel out of reach.

Do you value your skills and time?

Do you hesitate to charge what you are worth?

For example, *Kainaz Messman Harchandrai*, the co-founder of Theobroma, overcame a brutal and life-threatening accident to start her own bakery business. She introduced high-quality, European-style patisseries to India, pricing them accordingly, and today, Theobroma has 78 outlets across the country.

Final Reflection

So, track your income, savings, expenses, be very specific about your financial goals, express gratitude and avoid scarcity mindset. If money were a person, it would thrive in a relationship built on respect, gratitude and care. It would want to support you, celebrate your successes, and be a reliable person in your life.

Treat money like a trusted companion, not an enemy or a fleeting visitor. Build a relationship where both of you grow, thrive and create something meaningful together.

Money is not just a tool; it's an energy, a relationship and a mirror reflecting your mindset. Nurture it, value it and it will flow into your life abundantly. Remember, money isn't just a means to an end- it's a reflection of how you value yourself and the energy you bring to the world.

10
MINDFULNESS AND BEING PRESENT

> "The present moment is the only time over which we have dominion."
> – Thich Nhat Hanh

The Essence of Presence

In the era characterized by constant distractions and relentless pace, the ability to remain present has become both a challenge as well as a necessity. Mindfulness, the practice of anchoring oneself in the current moment, offers a pathway to enhanced well-being, deeper connections and a more fulfilling life.

How many of you feel that you are living the same life over the years? It has become very easy to predict the future as your entire attention is either on the past or on the future. Energy stays where your focus is, and unfortunately it is never on the present. Hence your future will exactly be like your past only and days will pass by. It is utmost necessary to be mindful, engage your energy in the present to achieve a brighter future.

Understanding Mindfulness

Mindfulness is the deliberate focus of attention in the present moment, acknowledging the thoughts, feelings and sensations without judgment. It involves a conscious awareness of the, *"here and now,"* rather than ruminating on the past or anticipating the future. This practice allows a deeper connection with oneself and the surrounding world, enhancing clarity and emotional balance.

Neuroscience behind Mindfulness

Engaging in mindfulness practices induces measurable changes in the brain and strengthens the functions such as decision making, attention and self regulation. It reduces the size and activity of amygdala thus decreases stress and anxiety levels. It also enhances the connectivity between the brain regions, promoting better integration and communication within the brain.

These neural adaptations contribute to improved emotional regulation, increased focus and greater capacity for empathy.

Spiritual Perspectives on Presence

Buddhism encourages living fully in the present moment as a means to attain enlightenment and inner peace.

Christianity advocates for mindfulness in daily life as reflected in the teachings of being watchful and present.

Sufism highlights the significance of presence *(hudur)* in experiencing divine love and connection.

These traditions underscore that presence is integral to spiritual growth and a deeper understanding of oneself and the universe.

Benefits of Being Present

Studies show that the four major challenges that people encounter while practicing mindfulness is distractibility, loneliness, negative self talk and lack of meaning or purpose in life; whereas the four pillars of it are awareness, connection, insights and purpose.

Cultivating mindfulness and presence yields numerous benefits. By focusing on the present, individuals can alleviate anxiety related to past regrets or future uncertainties. Being fully present improves communication and deepens connection with others and in return enhances your relationships. Mindfulness enhances focus, improves efficiency in tasks, minimizes distractions and increases productivity. It also leads to greater emotional balance and overall life satisfaction.

For example, a *couple* who were experiencing frequent misunderstandings began practicing mindful listening during conversations. By fully attending to each other's words without interruption or judgment, they improved their communication and strengthened their relationship.

In another case, a *parent* noticed they were often distracted during time with their child. By practicing mindfulness, they became more engaged during interactions, fostering a deeper bond and creating a more supportive environment for their child's development.

A *professional* facing high workplace stress started incorporating brief mindfulness exercise into his day, like taking short breaks, grounding himself into the present moment helped reduce anxiety as well as improved productivity.

Research has found that if an individual focuses on mindful *eating*, like focusing on each bite, savoring flavors and paying attention to hunger developed a healthier relationship with food, leading to much improved digestion and weight management.

A recent article emphasizes the importance of mindful practices during travel. It stated, *"There's nothing worse than visiting somewhere beautiful but being distracted,"* and, *"There's nothing better than being fully present for all the small joys you find in the details."*

Practical Strategies to Cultivate Mindfulness

Mindful breathing

Dedicate a few minutes daily to focus solely on your breath, observing each inhale and exhale.

Body scan meditation

Progressively direct attention to different parts of your body, noting sensations and tensions.

Mindful Observation

Engage fully with your surroundings, paying close attention to sights, sounds and texture without judgment.

Mindful eating

Savor each bite during meals, focus on flavors, textures and the act of eating without distractions.

Digital Detox

Allocate specific times to disconnect from electronic world, allowing engagement with the present moment.

Mindful listening

Practice active listening in conversations, giving your full attention without interrupting or even planning your response.

Integrate it in routine activities and daily tasks such as brushing teeth, washing dishes, walking by fully engaging in the activity at hand. Also, set aside time each day for reflection or meditation to reinforce practices.

Overcoming Challenges

It's natural for the mind to wander. Gently redirect your focus back to the present without self criticism. It may also bring up uncomfortable emotions. Acknowledge them without judgments and allow them to pass naturally.

Embracing the present

Mindfulness and being present are transformative practices that enrich life by fostering a deeper connection to oneself and the world. By integrating it into daily routines, you can experience enhanced well being, improved relationships and a more profound sense of fulfillment.

Remember, the journey is personal and ongoing. Embrace each moment as it comes and allow the practice to unfold in your life naturally.

"When we get too caught up in the busyness of the world, we lose connection with one another, and ourselves."-Jack Kornfield

11

FINDING A PURPOSE IN LIFE

> "The meaning of life is to find your gift. The purpose of life is to give it away."
> – Pablo Picasso

Finding your purpose is one of the most profound and fulfilling journeys you can embark on. It's not about chasing external validation or blindly following societal expectations- it's actually about uncovering the unique reason you exist and aligning your actions with that deeper calling.

What is Purpose?

It is the guiding star of your life. It is the reason you wake up excited in the morning, a torchbearer to live, the deeper meaning behind your actions and the anchor that keeps you grounded in challenging times.

Purpose vs. Goals

Goals are specific milestones; purpose is the overarching reason driving those goals.

Purpose is Personal

It doesn't have to be grand or world-changing—it just needs to be meaningful to you.

For example, marriage can be a goal or a milestone for many, but the purpose of marriage differs for each individual. For some, it may be companionship or emotional support, while for others, it may represent economic stability, responsibility, social security, or procreation.

Mahatma Gandhi found his life's purpose in serving humanity and advocating for non-violence, which became the driving force behind India's independence movement—a goal that many aspired to.

The Science behind Purpose

Studies suggest that having a purpose activates the brain's reward system, releasing dopamine- a feel-good hormone. People with purpose exhibit lower stress levels and better mental health. Moreover, purpose driven individuals are more focused and determined. The prefrontal cortex, responsible for decision making and goal setting, becomes more active.

Victor Frankl, a psychiatrist and Holocaust survivor, emphasized in *Man's search for meaning* that having a clear purpose was the difference between survival and giving up in the harshest conditions.

Quantum Physics behind Energy and Purpose

Quantum physics teaches us that everything in the universe is made up of energy, including your thoughts, emotions, intentions as well as goals. Positive thoughts and purpose driven actions align us with higher vibrational frequencies which aids in attracting people, opportunities and circumstances that resonate with that energy.

Spiritual Insights

Every spiritual tradition highlights the role of purpose as a divine assignment or cosmic duty.

In **Hinduism**, the concept of dharma emphasizes one's duty and moral responsibility in the larger order of the universe.

In **Buddhism,** purpose is tied in achieving inner peace and enlightenment by following the eightfold path.

Christianity teaches that purpose is God's plan for each individual, guiding them to serve others selflessly, as emphasized in the Bible.

Islam views purpose as fulfilling Allah's will and contributing to humanity with sincerity and devotion.

Cosmic Purpose: You Are Stardust

Astrophysics reveals that every element in our body originated from stars that exploded billions of years ago.

We are deeply connected to the universe in the most profound way. Our existence is not random—it is part of a vast, universal story.

Carl Sagan, the renowned astrophysicist, once said, *"We are a way for the universe to know itself. Every soul has a role to play in the grand cosmic dance."*

How to Discover Your Purpose

Finding your purpose is an evolving journey, and certain steps can guide you along the way. Start by asking yourself: *Who am I called to serve?* When you step into a purpose rooted in service, your life immediately gains meaning, and your brain lights up like a light bulb—a phenomenon known as the "helper's high," as described by *Tyler Cerny*.

Next, ask yourself: *What problems am I called to solve?* Finally, reflect on *how* you are meant to solve them. These questions can help you uncover a deeper sense of purpose and fulfillment.

Self Reflection

Ask yourself questions such as *what brings me joy? What am I naturally good at? What problems do I feel called to solve?*

Identify your values

Your core values act as a compass guiding your purpose.

Explore and experiment

Try new experiences, meet new people and step out of your comfort zone.

Pay attention to what energizes you

Purpose is a driven force, it always feels energizing, not draining. Ask *what am I passionate about? What am I skilled at? How can I use my passions and skills to help others?*

Sometimes, obstacles prevent you from discovering your purpose. Fear of failure can keep you stuck in inaction. Also, comparing your journey to others can cloud your vision. Societal or familial expectations can distract you from your authentic path.

Aligning Purpose with Daily Life

Once you gain clarity about your purpose, integrate it into your daily life. Align your goals with what truly fulfills you. Set your priorities straight and in order. Start living intentionally and consciously—every small decision should contribute to your larger vision.

Purpose isn't static; it evolves with you, so stay adaptable.

For example, Elon Musk aligns his purpose of advancing sustainable energy and space exploration with every project he undertakes.

Remember, your purpose isn't just about you—it often involves contributing to something larger. Start by building meaningful relationships, supporting causes you believe in, and sharing your knowledge and resources with others.

The Intersection of Purpose and Happiness

Purpose isn't always easy. It requires effort, sacrifice and resilience. But a purpose driven life leads to deeper happiness and contentment. It provides clarity during challenging times and brings a sense of accomplishment beyond material success.

You are the Author of your Story

Finding your purpose isn't a onetime discovery, it's an ongoing process. Life will present opportunities, challenges and moments of clarity along the way. Trust your journey, stay open to growth and most importantly, listen to your inner voice. Your purpose doesn't have to be extraordinary in the eyes of others. If it feels right in your heart and brings light to your soul, you have found it. Start today and live with purpose, and let your life be your message.

12
MEETING GOALS WITH YOUR NEEDS: THE BALANCE BETWEEN AMBITION AND WELL-BEING

> "Success without fulfillment is the ultimate failure."
> – Tony Robbins

Understanding the Balance between Goals and Needs

In today's fast paced world, people often chase their goals without considering whether they align with their true needs. Sometimes the reason the goals are not achieved is solely because they do not match your needs. Goals are external milestones- like earning promotion, buying a house or reaching a fitness target. Needs, on the other hand, are internal- like emotional well being, security, connection and self acceptance.

When our goals are disconnected from our core needs, they often lead to burnout, dissatisfaction and emptiness. True success lies in aligning your external goals with your internal needs.

Goal example: Becoming the CEO of a company

Need example: Feeling valued, secure, respected and having a sense of purpose

When your goals fulfill your needs, success becomes sustainable and meaningful or else you sabotage it.

Maslow's Hierarchy of Needs

Abraham Maslow's hierarchy of needs offers a powerful framework for understanding the balance between goals and needs.

Physiological needs

Food, water and shelter.

Safety needs

Security, stability and health.

Love and Belonging

Relationships, friendships and intimacy.

Esteem needs

Respect, recognition and self-confidence.

Self-actualization

Achieving your full potential, personal growth and purpose.

If your goals are misaligned with your level of needs, you may feel unfulfilled despite achieving them. For example, pursuing wealth(esteem need) when your emotional health(safety need) is neglected can lead to stress and dissatisfaction.

7 Chakras, 7 Needs: Aligning Energy Centers for Fulfillment

The human body is not just a physical entity; it is also a vessel of energy. Ancient Indian wisdom describes the 7 chakras as energy centers, each governing specific aspects of our physical, emotional and spiritual well being. When these chakras are balanced, energy flows freely, aligning your needs.

Root chakra(Muladhara)

The needs are safety, stability, financial security and basic survival. When balanced it provides a sense of grounding, safety and resilience is life's challenges.

Sacral Chakra (Svadhisthana)

The needs are of changes, exploration, creativity, experiences and pleasure. When balanced, it allows for joy, creative expression and fulfilling relationships.

Solar Plexus (Manipura)

The needs are self-esteem, confidence, control and personal power. When balanced, it empowers decision making and confidence.

Heart Chakra (Anahata)

The needs are love, compassion, connection and emotional balance. It governs your capacity for love and compassion, for yourselves and others.

Throat Chakra (Vishuddha)

The needs are authentic communication, self expression and truth. This governs the ability to speak your truth and express yourself openly.

Third Eye Chakra (Ajna)

The needs are intuition, clarity, inner wisdom and serving. It helps you help, see beyond illusions and connect with your inner truth.

Crown Chakra (Sahasrara)

The needs are spiritual growth, self transcendence and doing nothing. It represents pure awareness and enlightenment.

These aren't just ancient philosophy- they represent fundamental human needs which are essential to fulfill our goals, create balance, purpose and harmony.

Aligning your Goals with Your Core Values

Ask yourself, *"Why do I want to achieve this goal?"*. Identify your core values. Values like family, creativity, independence or security should guide your goals. Ensure every goal addresses an emotional, physical or spiritual need.

To exemplify, if your goal is to start a business and for that introspect what your core needs are. Is it freedom, creativity or financial security. If your goal only focuses on profit, but neglects creativity and freedom, you may feel trapped despite financial success.

When a goal lacks emotional or intrinsic value, you quickly return to an unsatisfied state. Intrinsic goals are usually driven by personal growth, relationships and fulfillment like learning a skill for self improvement. On the contrary, extrinsic goals are driven by external rewards like money, fame or approval like buying luxury items for social validation. Studies suggest that intrinsic goals lead to long term happiness, while extrinsic goals provide short term satisfaction.

Spiritual Perspectives on Goals and Needs

In **Hinduism**, the *Bhagavad Gita* emphasizes *Nishkama Karma*—pursuing goals without attachment to the outcome, focusing instead on purpose and the intent behind actions.

In **Buddhism**, goals should align with *right intention* and *right effort* to cultivate inner peace and fulfillment.

In **Christianity**, the Bible states, *"Seek first the kingdom of God, and all these things will be added to you."*

In **Islam**, aligning goals with *Tawakkul* (trust in God's plan) ensures peace and balance in achieving both worldly and spiritual aspirations.

These spiritual traditions emphasize that goals should serve your well-being, not just your ego.

Practical Strategies to Align Goals with Needs

Define your *"Why"* and ask yourself, *"Why do I want to achieve this goal?"*

Ensure that your goals are **specific, measurable, achievable, relevant, and time-bound.**

Evaluate your emotional needs by asking, *"Will this goal fulfill my deeper needs for security, love, or growth?"*

Prioritize self-care—no goal is worth sacrificing your mental, emotional, or physical health.

Celebrate small wins. Acknowledge progress and align your celebrations with meaningful milestones.

The *law of attraction* states that what we focus on, we attract. When you set goals aligned with your deepest needs, your energy becomes magnetic to success.

Role of Goals and Needs in Career and Relationships

In terms of relationships, it's very critical to know the needs of your partner, friends and colleagues in order to build a beautiful connection. By knowing their first three needs itself, talking about it and taking actions for it can help resolve any issues. It is not necessary to match your needs with them, just fulfilling each other's needs can aid a better compatibility.

However, when it comes to career and finances, it is essential to evaluate one's needs and goals. It's important to introspect and ask yourself, *"What do I want more at this stage of my life?"*

For example, if someone aims to achieve a certain level of success in their career and earn more money, they should prioritize growth and change over comfort and love.

The Sweet Spot of Balance

Success isn't about reaching every goal- it's about reaching the right goals. Goals that satisfy your physical, emotional and spiritual needs create a life of balance, joy and meaning. So, don't chase goals blindly. Align them with your values and core needs and celebrate the journey, not just the destination. When your goals serve your needs, you don't just achieve success, you experience completeness and fulfillment.

13
HEALTH, ENERGY AND ABUNDANCE

*W*hen we think of abundance, our minds often drift towards wealth or success. Nevertheless, true abundance is incomplete without vibrant physical health and boundless energy. Your body is the vessel through which you experience life, and the state of your health significantly impacts how you feel, think and manifest abundance in life. There is a profound connection between physical health, emotional well being and the energy that fuels your journey towards abundance.

The Body as the Reflection of Mind

Have you ever noticed how stress can give you a headache or how joy can make you feel light and energetic? Your body is deeply connected to your thoughts and emotions. Negative emotions such as suppressed anger, resentment or guilt can manifest as physical ailments over time. For instance:

Anger is linked to liver dysfunction, high blood pressure and migraines. In traditional Chinese medicine(TCM), the liver is associated with the flow of emotions.

Sadness or grief is often associated with weakened lung function or fatigue.

Fear or anxiety is tied to kidney issues, insomnia or digestive problems.

Excessive empathy or heartbreak can strain the heart and the cardiovascular system.

Worry, fear and guilt cause indigestion, bloating, ulcers or irritable bowel syndrome(IBS).

Financial stress leads to lower back pain whereas *emotional burden* leads to upper back pain as the back represents support, whether physical, emotional or financial thus creating tension in the muscle or spine.

Difficulty in receiving or giving love manifests as joint pain in arms and hands as they symbolize how you connect and share with the world.

Fear of change, feeling stuck or insecurities lead to knee pain or swelling in legs as they are symbolic of movement and progress.

Do you know that when you *can't express your anger*, that is when your throat chakra is suppressed, you get frequent throat infections or catch cold flu very easily.

Dr. Gabor Mate, renowned physician and author describes cases where people suppress anger or overextend themselves to please people, leading to autoimmune disorders.

These patterns aren't mere coincidences; they are evidence of mind-body connection. What you suppress mentally finds expression in your physical body. If you find yourself frequently unwell or fatigued, it's worth reflecting on your mental and emotional state. Are you carrying unprocessed emotions or toxic thoughts? By addressing these, you not only heal emotionally but also create a healthier physical state.

Physical Health as a Catalyst for Abundance

When you feel physically healthy, you radiate energy. This vitality is contagious and directly influences how you approach your goals and relationships. Physical health increases your clarity and focus enabling better decision making. It also provides you with sustained energy levels that helps you tackle challenges with resilience and enthusiasm. Feeling good in your body boosts self esteem making you feel capable of achieving anything.

Healing the Body with Mindful Practices

Improving your physical health doesn't have to be complicated. Often, small consistent changes can have a significant impact. Mindful eating, exercises and movement, breath work and meditation and adequate rest helps in boosting good health.

Emotional Healing for Physical Health

Emotions are energy in motion. Suppressing them creates blockages that can lead to physical ailments. Healing begins with acknowledging and releasing these emotions. Therapy, counseling and forgiveness aids in releasing them. Remember, abundance flows when you are not weighed down by emotional baggage.

Closing Thoughts

The mind and body are mirrors of one another. They are deeply interconnected and multifaceted, shaped by your thoughts, energy and actions. Your body is the foundation of your life. Treat it with love and care, and it will reward you with vitality and energy needed to achieve your dreams. Abundance starts from within and by nurturing your health, you set the stage for a truly fulfilling and abundant life. The more you care for your body, the more it empowers you to live a life full of joy, energy and purpose.

14

DECISION MAKING

*Y*our quality of life depends on the decision you make. Whatever struggles you have today are because of the decisions you made in the past at that time. Decision making is an art and a science -a fundamental skill that shapes the quality of your lives. Each choice we make, whether monumental or seemingly insignificant, has the power to steer you towards your success, fulfillment and growth, or lead you to stagnation and regret. Understanding how to make effective decisions is not just a skill; it is a cornerstone of living an intentional and abundant life.

Importance of Clarity

At the heart of good decision-making lies clarity. When your mind is cluttered with conflicting thoughts, fears and doubts, you will always vibrate in a very poor frequency hence your ability to discern the best path forward diminishes because you will attract poor opportunities only according to the universal law of energy. This might lead to stress resulting in getting stuck in the past and creating the same cycle for the future. Clarity arises when you are connected to your goals, values and purpose. It is the compass that guides you through the complexities of life.

Making Decisions Right:
Personally right or wrong

Decisions are always personally right or wrong. Never ask others for decisions because decisions are never globally right. They should be right or wrong according to you.

Never Take Decisions, Make Decisions

Decisions are always made based on calculated costs, benefits and emotions. Intentionally made decisions always serve your purpose.

Every Decision Has a Cost

Each decision that you make has a cost. It can be either emotional, physical, financial or social cost. For example, the decision to get married has emotional, financial and social costs. These costs can be predictable or unpredictable. Cost is a reality because every decision has some cost.

The Role of Emotions

Emotions play a significant role in decision making, often acting as both a catalyst and a barrier. While emotions can provide valuable insight, they can also cloud judgment when left unchecked. One of the most debated aspects of decision making is the balance between intuition and logic.

Intuition refers to your subconscious mind processing information faster than your conscious awareness; while logic, on the other hand, relies on reason, analysis and facts. Successful decision makers learn to integrate both.

Overcoming Decision Paralysis: Formula of Right Decision Making

Asking Costs

If you want to ask others, don't ask the decision, ask what the costs of this decision from the other person's perspective can be.

Write Benefits and Costs

List all the potential benefits and costs associated with your decision. If you anticipate paying the costs with regret, the decision may not be the right one. However, if you are willing to accept the costs without hesitation, it could be the right choice.

For example, if you plan to invest ₹10,000 in stocks, consider the potential loss. Ask yourself, *"Am I prepared to lose the entire ₹10,000?"* If the answer is yes, then proceed with confidence.

Willingness and Capacity

It is important to have both capacity as well as willingness for the decision.

Unpredictable costs

A few costs cannot be predicted from the beginning. So, it is important to be mentally prepared for those too.

Importance of Time

Decisions should be worth the benefits at that particular period of time.

Values and Needs

Choose your costs based on your values and needs. Remember, the cost of bad decisions is always more than the cost of right decision.

Take Action: Sell first, Make later, Fail fast

One thing that stops all of us from taking action is perfection and fear of failure. Remember, Perfection is the enemy of execution. Whenever you want to start something, apply this principle. When you sell or declare first, your frequency goes up, so you are bound to work very hard. If you fail, you should fail fast, as the thought of it will get removed from your mind fast and you can start focusing on the next.

To exemplify, it has been noticed in the diamond industry that the miners take the deposit first promising to deliver diamonds and then start digging everywhere.

The Power of Small Decisions

It's important to remember that life is shaped not just by big decisions, but also by small daily ones. What you eat, how you spend your time and who you interact with, may seem trivial, but over time, these choices compound to create the life you experience. Even if the decision doesn't yield the results you hoped for, it can teach you valuable lessons and redefine your decision-making process.

Spiritual Perspective on Decision making

In **Hinduism**, the *Bhagavad Gita* illustrates how Lord Krishna advises Arjuna on the battlefield to make decisions aligned with his higher purpose and duty, without attachment to the outcome.

In **Christianity**, the Bible encourages believers to seek divine wisdom before making decisions.

In **Islam**, believers are guided to practice *Istikhara* (seeking Allah's guidance) and *Shura*(mutual consultation) for informed and collective decision-making.

In **Buddhism**, *sati*(mindfulness) and the *Noble Eightfold Path,* particularly right intention and right action, help individuals make ethical and conscious decisions.

In **Jainism**, the principle of *Anekantavada*(multiple perspectives) encourages considering different viewpoints before making a decision.

Final Thoughts

Decisions are building blocks of life. Each one you make is an opportunity to move closer to your goals, values and dreams. By cultivating clarity, balancing intuition with logic and embracing both successes and lessons, you can master the art of decision making and create a life that reflects the abundance within you.

15

THE POWER OF LETTING GO AND FORGIVENESS

> "To forgive is to set a prisoner free and discover that the prisoner was you."
> – Lewis B. Smedes

The Weight We Carry

Imagine walking through life with a heavy backpack filled with stones. Each stone represents resentment, anger, guilt, and pain from past experiences. The longer you carry this backpack, the more it weighs you down—physically, emotionally, and spiritually. Letting go and forgiving is not about excusing others or forgetting what happened; it's about releasing this burden so you can walk freely into your future.

Forgiveness and letting go are not merely acts of kindness toward others—they are acts of liberation for yourself.

By forgiving others, you are actually doing yourself a favor. Unhealed past traumas leave deep imprints on your subconscious mind, which can unconsciously manifest in your surroundings and future. Energy flows where your focus is, and if your attention remains on unresolved battles in your mind, they will continue to shape your reality.

For example, parents are often our first significant relationships. Unresolved issues or criticisms toward them can unknowingly manifest in your relationships with friends, colleagues, or even a romantic partner. Additionally, holding onto negative emotions can store stress in your body's cells, potentially leading to physical ailments.

Understanding Forgiveness: What It Is and What It Isn't

Forgiveness is not weakness

Forgiving someone does not mean you condone their actions or let them off the hook. It means you are strong enough to release the power they have over your emotions.

Forgiveness is a choice

It is an active decision to free yourself from all the emotional chains of resentment and hurt.

Forgiveness is for you, not them

Often, the person who hurt you may not even remember or acknowledge their actions. Forgiveness is about your healing, not theirs.

The Science behind Letting Go

Studies show that holding onto anger and resentment increases stress hormones like cortisol which can lead to physical health issues such as high blood pressure, weakened immunity and chronic illness. When you forgive, your brain releases dopamine and serotonin promoting feelings of relief and peace.

Universal Energy and the Power of Letting Go

"The moment you let go, you make space for the universe to work its magic."

When we cling to anger, resentment, or fear, we block the natural flow of energy, causing stagnation that can lead to emotional fatigue, mental fog, and even physical ailments such as headaches, body pain, or chronic illness.

Think of a flowing river—when debris gets stuck, the water stagnates, creating an unhealthy, murky pool. Similarly, unresolved emotions block the energy within us, preventing personal growth and peace.

Spiritual Perspectives on Forgiveness and Letting Go

Across spiritual traditions, forgiveness is seen as a path to inner peace and divine connection.

In Hinduism, *Kshama* (forgiveness) is one of the highest virtues. The *Bhagavad Gita* emphasizes the importance of releasing resentment to achieve spiritual liberation.

In Buddhism, Buddha taught, *"Holding onto anger is like drinking poison and expecting the other person to die."* Letting go of anger and resentment is central to achieving Nirvana.

In Christianity, the Bible repeatedly emphasizes forgiveness. The Lord's Prayer includes, *"Forgive us our trespasses, as we forgive those who trespass against us."*

In Islam, the Quran teaches, *"But if you pardon and overlook—then Allah is Forgiving and Merciful."*

In Jainism, forgiveness is a daily practice through *Michhami Dukkadam*, where followers seek forgiveness for any harm caused, knowingly or unknowingly.

The Emotional Freedom of Letting Go

Letting go doesn't mean forgetting. It means releasing emotional attachment to a painful memory. Often, we are our harshest critics. Forgiving yourself for past mistakes is a crucial step towards healing. Acceptance is the key. Accept the past for what it was whether right or wrong. Acceptance does not mean approval; it means acknowledging reality and moving forward. To add to this, understanding that people act from their own wounds makes forgiveness way easier.

Real Life Examples

Nelson Mandela spent 27 years in prison, yet he emerged not with bitterness, but with forgiveness. He said, *"As I walked out of the door toward the gate that led to freedom, I knew that if I didn't leave my bitterness and hatred behind, I would still be in prison."*

Oprah Winfrey openly shares her journey of forgiving her mother and others who hurt her during her childhood. She emphasizes that forgiveness was a crucial turning point in both her personal and professional success.

After the devastating loss of his family in the 2015 Charleston church shooting, *Chris Singleton* publicly forgave the shooter. His forgiveness became a powerful global message of love triumphing over hate.

Some Practical Steps to Forgive and Let Go

Acknowledge the pain. Pen down your feelings in a journal. Be honest about how the hurt has affected you. Understanding the other person's perspective is the first step. It may not be easy, try to understand what may have driven their actions. Practice compassion and empathy.

Realize that everyone carries their own wounds. Focus on the present moment. Don't let the past rob you of your present joy. If needed, seek support, talk to a counselor, coach or a trusted friend if it feels overwhelming.

A Life Set Free

Forgiveness doesn't just heal you; it creates a ripple effect. When you forgive, you model peace, compassion and strength for those around you. Families heal when grudges are released. Friendships deepen when apologies are accepted. Work environments improve when past misunderstandings are cleared up. Forgiveness is not a onetime event; it's an ongoing practice. Old wounds may resurface, but each time they do, you have a choice again. When you let go, you clear space in your heart for love, joy and peace.

Imagine a life unburdened by the past, a life where your energy is directed towards growth, happiness and connection.

Remind yourself: *"Forgiveness is my gift to myself. I am free. I choose peace, power and freedom."*

16
THE LAW OF ATTRACTION- MANIFESTING YOUR BEST LIFE

> "What you think, you become. What you feel you attract. What you imagine, you create."
> – Buddha

The Energy of Your Thoughts

The law of attraction operates on a simple yet profound principle: like attracts like. It suggests that your thoughts, emotions and beliefs have the power to shape your reality. Whether consciously or unconsciously, you are constantly manifesting your experiences through your mental focus and emotional energy.

Imagine your mind to be a magnet, attracting people, opportunities and situations that align with your thoughts and feelings. This law isn't magic- it's a compilation of psychological principles, quantum physics, neuroscience and ancient spiritual wisdom.

The Science Behind the Law of Attraction

Just like the law of gravity, the law of attraction exists. You do not need to fully understand how it works, but believing in its power is essential.

Every matter—living or non-living—consists of energy. You might recall from your school days that mitochondria produce energy for the cell. Additionally, energy can neither be created nor destroyed; it can only be transformed from one form to another.

The Laws of Karma also reinforce this principle, stating that whatever actions you take will return to you—either in this life or another—since the soul is immortal, while the body is temporary, like clothes that you change.

Have you ever felt an instant positive connection upon meeting someone for the first time? This is because your soul, being energy, recognizes familiar energy—even if it stems from a past life. Similarly, your *kundli* (birth chart) is believed to be a reflection of past actions and karma.

Newton's Third Law states that every action has an equal and opposite reaction. This supports the idea that everything is composed of energy, radiating at specific frequencies that shape reality.

Your goals, emotions, and desires are also forms of energy. Every room carries the frequency of emotions, desires, and aspirations. Aligning yourself with the right frequency is crucial to attracting what you seek—just like tuning a radio to the perfect station to hear your favorite music.

Neuroscience and the Reticular Activating System (RAS)

Your brain has a powerful filtering mechanism called the Reticular Activating System (RAS), which focuses on what you consistently think about. For example, if you buy a red car, you suddenly start noticing red cars everywhere. This isn't a coincidence—it's your brain filtering reality based on your focus.

The brain is neuroplastic, meaning it continuously rewires itself based on repetitive thoughts, beliefs, and external influences. This adaptability allows you to shape your perception and experiences through intentional focus.

Cognitive Behavioral Therapy (CBT) is a proven method that helps reframe negative thought patterns, reinforcing positive beliefs and supporting manifestation.

When your brain rewires itself toward a particular goal, it strengthens conviction, which leads to devotion and ultimately results in transformation.

How Does the Law of Attraction Work?

Why do some people achieve great success while others don't? It's because, consciously or unconsciously, they are attracting the right things into their lives.

According to the law of energy, everything is made up of energy, and at the energy level, all are one. If you want to attract something, you need to tune into the right frequency so that your energy aligns with it. In essence, you are attracting a part of something that is already within you.

Think about your last birthday—you likely remember it clearly. But do you remember the day before or after? Probably not. That's because emotions were attached to your birthday, making it more significant. Similarly, when your brain rewires itself toward a goal, it generates emotions of conviction, which lead to devotion and ultimately transformation.

When the right emotions and interpretations come together, they form the right affirmations, which naturally lead you to the right people and opportunities. For example, *Dhirubhai Ambani* used to drink tea worth ₹500 while his friends drank ₹50 tea at a stall. He did this to surround himself with successful businesspeople, aligning himself with the right associations.

Ultimately, the right emotions, affirmations, and associations lead to the right actions. When your frequency aligns with your desires, you begin attracting the right people, opportunities, and direction in life.

For example, the famous Indian singer *Diljit Dosanjh* once mentioned in an interview that from a very young age, he knew he was going to be famous. He would look in the mirror and visualize a crowd cheering for him. His strong emotions, visualization, conviction, and actions turned that belief into reality.

The Law of Attraction is not just about wishful thinking, daydreaming, or repeating affirmations. True manifestation happens when you convince your mind of the real value of something by dedicating your time, money, and attention to it—keeping it close, aligning your beliefs, emotions, and thoughts with it, and taking the necessary actions to make it a reality. That's when the magic happens.

The Spiritual Roots of the Law of Attraction

In **Hinduism**, the *Bhagavad Gita* emphasizes the power of intention and action:

"You are what you believe in. You become that which you believe you can become."

A well-known story from the *Satyanarayan Katha* illustrates this concept. A priest once asked a businessman, whose boat was filled with gold, what he was carrying. The businessman, either out of humility or disbelief, replied that his boat contained *belpatras*—sacred leaves offered to Lord Shiva. Upon his response, he suddenly noticed that all his gold had turned into those very leaves. This story highlights the power of words, belief, and perception in shaping reality.

The Bhagavad Gita also states:

"Paripatrena, Pariprashnena, and Sevaya"—*Through complete surrender, meaningful inquiry, and the right actions, true success is achieved.*

In **Buddhism**, Buddha taught the principle that *"mind precedes all"*, meaning our thoughts shape our reality.

In **Christianity**, the Bible reinforces the idea of asking with faith:

"Ask, and it will be given to you; seek, and you will find; knock, and the door will be opened to you." (Matthew 7:7)

In **Islam**, the *Quran* emphasizes *tawakkul* (trust in Allah), highlighting that strong intention, faith, and action work together to manifest one's desires.

Each of these spiritual traditions underscores the importance of **intention, focus, and belief** in manifesting outcomes, aligning closely with the principles of the Law of Attraction.

Conclusion

The law of attraction isn't just about wishful thinking— it's about setting intentions, attaching emotions, dedication and aligned actions. The universe responds to your energy, so align your thoughts, words, actions with your desired outcomes. Your mind is your most powerful tool. Use it wisely, dream boldly and act fearlessly.

17

HOW TRAVEL CHANGES YOUR MINDSET: TRAVEL LIKE A TRAVELER, NOT A TOURIST

"Travel isn't always about changing locations; sometimes it's about changing perspectives."

*T*ravel has the power to transform us– not just through places we visit, but through the way we experience them. The difference between a traveler and a tourist lies in their mindset. A tourist often follows checklist, rushing from one attraction to another, capturing moments on camera without actually enjoying them. A traveler, on the other hand, immerses themselves in their culture, their local delicacies, embraces the unknown and builds connections that lasts a lifetime. A tourist seeks comfort, follows guidebooks and sticks to attraction; whilst the traveler seeks connections, explores local paths and learns from the culture. A tourist sees the world from a distance; a traveler steps into it.

For example, *Anthony Bourdain*, the famous chef and travel documentarian, traveled not just to see, but experience. He sat with the locals, tasted authentic cuisines and listened to their stories instead of just sightseeing.

Embrace Slow Travel, Cultivate Cultural Respect and be Open to New Experiences

In our fast-paced world, slowing down is a luxury. A traveler understands the value of lingering longer in one place, exploring its hidden alleys and sitting in local cafes observing daily life. Wander without an agenda, spend more time, observe, understand and choose experiences to grow yourself mentally.

For example, *Elizabeth Gilbert*, author of *Eat, Pray, Love*, spent months in Italy, India and Indonesia. She didn't rush her travels; she immersed herself in each culture, which changed her life a lot.

A traveler respects the culture, traditions and values of the places they visit. They observe local customs, dress appropriately and understand the social norms. Try to understand the behavior of people, their way of giving respect, try to learn a few basic phrases of local language, support local businessman and follow cultural etiquette.

For example, in Japan bowing is a sign of respect. Try to adapt it and build a rapport. Travel is about connection, and respect is the bridge that builds it.

Step out of your comfort zone, eat food you haven't eaten before, talk to strangers and say yes to spontaneous plans. Learn to let go of unnecessary worries.

Jack Kerouac's on the Road is a book that shows reflection of a journey through self discovery.

Travel Mindfully

Mindfulness is about fully present. A traveler practices mindfulness by appreciating the little details. Pause and observe your surroundings. Focus on the present moment and find joy in small experiences. It reduces stress and enhances memory retention.

Bhutan follows a *Gross National Happiness* policy, prioritizing happiness, sustainable tourism and mindfulness through its natural beauty.

Travel and Mindset Transformation

When you travel, your mind is exposed to new sights, sound, culture and people. These experiences challenge your existing beliefs, broaden your perspectives and allow you to see the world and yourself from a fresh lens. You are forced to adapt, solve problems and embrace uncertainty which naturally builds resilience and a growth mindset.

For example, a solo traveler navigating through an unfamiliar city learns independence, resourcefulness and confidence. These skills extend travel into everyday life. The mindset becomes stronger and more adaptable.

When you witness the beauty of a sunset in the mountains or experience the minimalism, you are reminded of small joys. Travel makes you grateful for what you have and present in the now. Natural places like mountains, beaches, forests have higher vibrational frequencies that naturally heal your energy. Even the chaotic energy of the bustling city affects your energetic state.

Travel often puts you in a *flow state*- a mental state where time disappears, and you are fully immersed in the present situation.

Neuroscience of Travel

Travel isn't just an emotional or physical, it physically rewires your brain. Every time you experience something new while travelling, your brain forms new neural connections which broadens the horizons for creativity, problem solving abilities and emotional intelligence.

Practical Steps to Mindful Traveling

Travel with Intention

Before setting out on your journey, ask yourself, *"What do I hope to gain from this experience?"* Setting an intention adds depth and meaning to your travels.

Be Present

Immerse yourself fully in the moment. Put down your phone, observe your surroundings, and engage with the culture around you.

Embrace Uncertainty

Unexpected challenges are a natural part of travel. Instead of resisting them, see them as opportunities for growth and new perspectives.

Connect with Locals

Engage in conversations with locals—they can offer insights and stories that no guidebook can provide, enriching your travel experience.

Final Reflection: Travel as a Path to Growth

Travel isn't about ticking destinations off a checklist; it's about the experiences that shape you. Each place, person and moment carry energy and it has the power to heal, inspire and transform you. It's more about who you become in the process. When you travel like a traveler, you come back not just with souvenirs, but with stories, wisdom and a renewed perspective of life.

When you travel with intention, openness and mindfulness, you allow yourself to align with universal energy and expand your mindset in ways you never thought was possible.

Every journey is an opportunity for growth, connection and transformation. The world is your classroom, and every journey is an opportunity to discover the abundance within you.

18

HOW FOOD IMPACTS YOUR THINKING: THE MIND-BODY CONNECTION

*W*e often hear the phrase, "*You are what you eat*," but rarely do we realize that it applies not just to our physical health but also to our mental clarity, emotional well being and overall mindset. Food is more than just fuel to your body- it's a powerful influence on your brain, your thoughts and your mood.

The Gut-Brain Connection: Your Second Brain

The gut is often referred to as the "second brain" because it contains millions of neurons and produces about 90% of serotonin, the neurotransmitter responsible for regulating mood, sleep, and overall happiness.

An unhealthy diet high in processed foods, sugar, and unhealthy fats can cause inflammation in the gut, disrupting serotonin production and leading to brain fog, anxiety, or depression. On the other hand, a healthy diet supports gut health, enhances mood, and sharpens cognitive functions.

Scientific Insight

Ever felt *"hangry"* when you skipped a meal? That's your gut-brain connection in action. Neuroscientific research has shown that a well-balanced diet supports the growth of beneficial gut bacteria, which communicate with the brain via the vagus nerve and produce neurotransmitters that influence our thoughts and emotions.

Nutrients that Fuel Your Mind

Foods such as omega-3 fatty acids, antioxidants, B-vitamins and complex carbohydrates enhance mental clarity, focus, memory, cognitive function and emotional stability.

To exemplify, *Steve Jobs* was known for maintaining plant-based diet, which he believed contributed to his focus, creativity and emotional thinking.

Emotional healing and Mental Health

Your emotional state often influences your eating habits. During stressful times, many people crave sugary or fried foods which leads to over-eating. This can provide temporary relief because they provide a quick dopamine rush which is often followed by energy crash, and increased anxiety and can lead to guilt, irritability, mood swings and sluggishness. So always pause and ask yourself, *"Am I eating because I am hungry, bored or stressed?"*

Hydration and Brain Function

Water is essential for every cell in the body including your brain. Dehydration impacts focus, memory and mood. Drinking enough water helps flush toxins and maintain mental clarity.

Spiritual and Cultural Perspectives on Food

Different religions and cultures have long emphasized the connection between food and mindset.

In **Hinduism**, the concept of *Sattvic food* emphasizes purity, clarity and calmness.

Buddhism embarks on mindful eating, where gratitude and presence are key essence of every meal.

In **Islam**, fasting during Ramadan teaches discipline, gratitude and control.

In **Christianity** and **Jainism** too, certain periods of fasting and dietary restrictions emphasize spiritual growth and clarity.

Food isn't just physical; it carries energetic vibrations that affect your mental and spiritual well being.

Final Reflection

The food you consume doesn't just fill your belly, it shapes your thoughts, emotions and mindset. A diet rich in nutritious, balanced and mindful choices will not only nourish your body but also empower your mind. Every bite you take fuels your growth, clarity, creativity and emotional well being.

19
GRATITUDE AS A FOUNDATION

*I*magine your life as a house. The strength and stability of that house depend on its foundation. Gratitude is that foundation. When you build your life on gratitude, you create a sturdy structure that can weather any storm. Gratitude has the power to shift your focus from what you lack to what you already have, seeding a sense of peace, joy and fulfillment.

Understanding Gratitude: What it is and Why it Matters

Gratitude isn't just saying "thank you" when something good happens; it's a deeper appreciation for life's blessings, both big and small. You need to appreciate small money too to gain big. It's a conscious practice of recognizing the good that already exists in your life.

Why it Matters?

It rewires the brain for positivity. Scientific studies show that practicing gratitude activates the brain's reward pathways, making you feel happier and more content.

It reduces stress and anxiety, improving your mental and emotional well being.

It also helps you attract abundance. When you focus on the good, you begin to see more good in your life. It isn't about ignoring life's challenges. It's about finding light even in dark times.

The Science Behind Gratitude: How it works

Research shows that gratitude has tangible benefits on your physical and mental health.

Boosts Happiness

Studies have proven that people who practice gratitude feel happier and more optimistic.

Reduces Stress

It helps lower cortisol, which is the hormone responsible for stress, and improves your ability to handle difficult situations.

Improves Sleep

It also aids to sleep better by shifting your focus in positive thinking.

Strengthens Relationships

Expressing gratitude to others fosters deeper connections and builds trust.

Imagine two people facing the same situation- a hectic day at work. One complains about the chaos, while the other feels grateful for having a job. The second person experiences less stress and a greater sense of purpose. Gratitude shapes how you respond to life.

The Gratitude Mindset: Shifting Your Focus

The world is full of distractions, and it's easy to focus on what's missing. But gratitude teaches us to focus on what is already present.

For that you need to start seeing challenges as opportunities for growth. Recognize even the smallest joys like a good meal, sunshine, a kind word from a stranger or as simple as waking up.

Instead of saying, *"I have to go to work,"* say, *"I get to go to work."* These small changes in perspectives create a ripple effect in your mindset.

Practicing Gratitude During Challenges

It's easy to feel grateful when everything is going well. But true gratitude shines during difficult times. Life may not always give you what you want, but it often gives you what you need for growth.

So, the question is how to develop gratitude during challenges?

For example, how would you react if you lost your job? You'd likely feel disappointed, right? Thoughts like *"Why does this always happen to me?"* or *"How will I survive now?"* might flood your mind. Instead, try asking yourself, *"What can I learn from this?"* or *"How can I use this time to focus on my health, spend time with family, learn a new skill, or be grateful for the opportunities this change might bring?"*

There's a saying: *When a storm arises in the ocean, a fisherman can either sit and complain or use the time to sharpen their tools and prepare for calmer waters.*

Gratitude doesn't erase pain, but it helps you find hope and strength to move forward. Many people believe they are entitled only to positive experiences and that negative events are inherently wrong. But that isn't true—light and dark, sunrise and sunset, both exist together. Life is a balance of opposites, and accepting both positive and negative experiences is key to resilience.

For example, a strong personality may come with a degree of aggressiveness. While this might seem negative, it can also be a lesson in self-awareness and emotional control, shaping a better future. The real issue is that people often avoid taking action on things within their control while trying to control things that aren't. This leads to frustration and disappointment. True strength comes from acknowledging one's flaws and working with them, rather than resisting them.

How many of you believe that you'll start thinking positively *only* when your problems disappear? The truth is, problems never completely go away—they are a constant part of life.

A helpful technique is *Negative Time Boxing*—a method where you set aside a specific, limited amount of time to consciously process negative emotions, thoughts, or frustrations. For example, you might allow yourself 30 minutes to vent, reflect, or feel upset about a situation. By acknowledging these emotions without letting them dominate your entire day, you maintain emotional balance and prevent negativity from derailing your overall well-being.

Gratitude as Magnet for Abundance

The law of attraction teaches that *"like attracts like."* When you focus on abundance and blessings, you attract more of the same in your life. Many spiritual philosophies teach that gratitude attracts more abundance. Expressing gratitude shifts one's energy to align with universal positivity. It is an energy amplifier.

As quoted by *Dr. Joe Vitale, "When you are grateful for what you have, you attract things to be more grateful for."*

Gratitude raises your energetic vibrations, aligning you with positive outcomes.

It is very important to celebrate other's success and their platform. There's a saying in India, *"Tenna ne kissi vaaste bhi tadi nahi mari, as vaaste, unha di bhi vaari nahi aa rahi,"* meaning if you don't clap for others, you will also not get a chance to celebrate and other's clapping for you.

Spiritual and Religious Aspects on Gratitude

In **Hinduism**, gratitude is considered a divine virtue and is deeply embedded in devotion, prayers, rituals, and *Karma Yoga*—the practice of performing actions selflessly while expressing gratitude to the divine for life's opportunities.

Similarly, in **Buddhism**, appreciation for the present moment and the interconnectedness of all beings is emphasized. Gratitude is expressed for all circumstances, recognizing that nothing exists independently.

In **Christianity**, the Bible states, *"Give thanks in all circumstances; for this is the will of God in Christ Jesus for you."*

In **Islam**, the Quran says, *"If you are grateful, I will surely increase you."* The frequent expression of *Alhamdulillah* reflects this practice of gratitude.

In **Judaism**, gratitude is deeply embedded in daily prayers, such as *Modeh Ani*, which is recited each morning to thank God for the gift of life.

Neuroscience and Gratitude

Practicing gratitude activates the brain's reward center, increasing dopamine and serotonin levels which boosts happiness and reduces cortisol levels decreasing stress. Regular gratitude rewires the brain to focus on positive experiences and creating lasting mental and emotional well being.

Closing Thoughts

Gratitude is a practice, not one-time action. The more you focus on what's good, the more goodness you will see. By choosing gratitude as your foundation, you construct a life that feels fulfilling, abundant and joyful, no matter what comes your way.

> *"Gratitude turns what we have into enough. It's not happiness that brings you gratitude, it's gratitude that brings you happiness."*

CONCLUSION

FINDING HAPPINESS, JOY AND LIVING THE LIFE YOU LOVE

> *"Joy does not simply happen to us. We have to choose joy and keep choosing it every day."*
> **– Henri Nouwen**

In a world often focused on achievement, external validation and societal expectations, personal joy stands as a deeply personal and unique experience- an art, not a formula. It's not merely the fleeting happiness from momentary pleasures but a profound state of being that comes from living authentically, aligning with one's values and embracing the present moment. It's an internal sense of contentment and fulfillment, independent of external circumstances. It's not about chasing happiness but cultivating a state of mind that allows joy to thrive naturally.

Happiness should be unconditional. Imagine the time when you were born. Did you need any goal, condition or a person to be happy? Then why can't this continue till the end of life?

"Your life is your masterpiece. Design it with intention, passion and courage."

Building a life you love isn't about chasing perfection or mimicking someone else's success- it's about aligning your daily actions, mindset and goals with your deepest values and aspirations. It requires clarity, self awareness, resilience and willingness to take ownership of your journey.

Building a fulfilling life begins with knowing what fulfillment means to you. It' not just about financial freedom, creative expression, nurturing relationships or contributing to a cause; it actually means living a balance of all HRCM; health, relationship, career and money. Identification of core values and aligning your goals with it, role of your mindset, embracing purpose and passion, balancing ambition and contentment, power of relationships, reflection and adaptation can catalyze in developing the life that you love.

Imagine your life as a blank canvas, and every decision, habit and relationship as a brushstroke. Don't wait for the perfect moment- start now.

As we come to an end of this transformative journey, it's essential to pause, reflect and recognize the power you now hold within you. *The Abundance Within* was never about external wealth, transient moments of happiness or superficial achievements- it was about limitless treasure already residing in you. Throughout this book, we've explored the power of mindset, self love, gratitude, forgiveness, mindfulness, physical and emotional well being, financial wellness and universal energy. Each chapter was a stepping-stone guiding you to understand that abundance isn't about having more- *it's about being more and creating more.*

The Journey Within Never Ends

Life isn't a straight road; it's an ever-evolving journey filled with highs and lows, challenges and victories. However, the tools that you have acquired through these pages- shifting your mindset, decluttering your life, embracing change -will always serve as your roadmap.

You Are the Creator of Your Reality

Every thought you think, every belief you hold and every action you take shapes your reality. Your mind is the soil, your beliefs are the seeds. and your actions are the sunlight and water. Nurture them well, and you'll create a garden of abundance, joy and fulfillment.

A Ripple Effect

When you live with abundance within, you become a light for others. Your energy will inspire those around you, creating a ripple effect of positivity, kindness and empowerment. Remember, change begins inside you, but its impact can echo across generations.

A Final Thought

You are enough. You are worthy of love, success, happiness and abundance- not because of what you do, but because of who you are.

Take a deep breath. Step forward with courage. Trust in the universe, trust in the process and most importantly trust in yourself.

Your journey doesn't end here- it's just the beginning.

With love, light and gratitude

Dr Parnavi Ganatra

www.ingramcontent.com/pod-product-compliance
Lightning Source LLC
LaVergne TN
LVHW041608070526
838199LV00052B/3041